Pathways of the Righteous

Written
by
Reb Moshe Steinerman

Edited by Elise Teitelbaum
& Rochel Steinerman

Reb Moshe Steinerman

iloveTorah Jewish Outreach Network

iloveTorah Jewish Publishing

First Published 2018

ISBN: 978-1-947706-04-0

Copyright: iloveTorah Jewish Publishing

www.ilovetorah.com

moshe@iloveTorah.com

All Rights reserved

Editor: Elise Teitelbaum & Rochel Steinerman

Artwork by Boris Shapiro

Reb Moshe Steinerman

ABOUT THE AUTHOR

Rabbi Moshe Steinerman grew up as a religious Jew, on the hillsides of Maryland. During his teenage years, Reb Moshe developed his talent for photography, while connecting to nature and speaking to *Hashem*. He later found his path through Breslov *chassidus*, while maintaining closeness to the *litvish* style of learning. He studied in the famous Baltimore *yeshiva*, *Ner Yisrael*, then married and moved to Lakewood, New Jersey. After settling down, he began to write his first book, *Kavanos Halev*, with the blessing of Rav Malkiel Kotler *Shlita*, *rosh yeshiva* of *Beis Medrash Gevoha*.

After establishing one of the first Jewish outreach websites, ilovetorah.com in 1996, Reb Moshe's teachings became popular amongst the full spectrum of Jews, ranging from the unaffiliated to ultra-Orthodox. His teachings, including hundreds of stories of tzaddikim, gained popularity due to the idea of drawing Jews together. Reb Moshe made *aliya* to *Tzfat*, Israel in 2003. Since then he has helped to bring back thousands of English-speaking Jews to their Jewish roots, through his thousands of online Jewish videos and audio lectures. His learning experience includes the completion of both Talmud Bavli and Yerushalmi as well as other important works.

In 2012, Reb Moshe, with his wife and children, moved to Jerusalem. He continued to teach and bring *Torah* insights to the world through his *Torah* learning series, which includes: Kavanos Halev (Meditations of the Heart), Tikkun Shechinah, Tovim Meoros (Glimpse of Light), Chassidus, Kabbalah & Meditation, Pesukei Torah (Passages of Torah), Yom Leyom (Day by Day), Prayers of the Heart, A Journey into Holiness, and The True Intentions of the Baal Shem Tov. Thousands have read the advice contained in these books, with life-changing results.

Reb Moshe Steinerman

In Memory of my father,

Reb Shlomo Zavel Ben Yaakov ZT"L

And all of the great souls of our people

I grew up in a house filled with the Torah learning of my father, who studied most of the day. Although there were no Jews in this remote part of Maryland, my father was a man of chesed to all people, and was known for his brilliance in Torah scholarship.

I want to say a special thank you to the Nikolsberg Rebbe and the Biala Rebbe for their encouragement and blessings. Most of all, I offer thanks to my wife, Rochel, for her faithful support.

Dedicated to my father-in-law Menachem Ben Reuven ZT"L. To my wife Rochel and to my children Shlomo Nachman, Yaakov Yosef, Gedalya Aharon Tzvi, Esther Rivka, Yeshiya Michel, Dovid Shmuel, Eliyahu Yisrael May it bring forth the light of your neshamos

Dear Reader,

Ilovetorah.com is a Jewish Outreach non-profit organization, with books and *Torah* classes available at low costs. Therefore, we appreciate your donation, to help Rabbi Moshe Steinerman and ilovetorah.com continue their work on behalf of the Jewish people. We also ask that you pass on these books to others once you are finished with them.

Thank you,

Reb Moshe Steinerman

www.ilovetorah.com

www.ilovetorah.com/donations

RABBINIC APPROVALS / HASKAMAHS

בס"ד

RABBI DOVID B. KAPLAN
RABBI OF WEST NEW YORK
5308 PALISADE AVENUE • WEST NEW YORK, NJ 07093
201-867-6859 • WESTNEWYORKSHUL@GMAIL.COM

דוד ברוך הלוי קאפלאן
רב ואב"ד דק"ק
וועסט ניו יארק

י' שבט ה'תשע"ז / February 6, 2017

Dear Friends,

Shalom and Blessings!

For approximately twenty years I have followed the works of Rabbi Moshe Steinerman, Shlit"a, a pioneer in the use of social media to encourage people and bring them closer to G-d.

Over the years Rabbi Steinerman has produced, and made public at no charge, hundreds of videos sharing his Torah wisdom, his holy stories, and his touching songs. Rabbi Steinerman has written a number of books, all promoting true Jewish Torah spirituality. Rabbi Steinerman's works have touched many thousands of Jews, and even spirituality-seeking non-Jews, from all walks of life and at all points of the globe.

Rabbi Steinerman is a tomim (pure-hearted one) in the most flattering sense of the word.

I give my full approbation and recommendation to all of Rabbi Steinerman's works.

I wish Rabbi Steinerman much success in all his endeavors.

May G-d bless Rabbi Moshe Steinerman, his wife, Rebbetzin Rochel Steinerman, and their beautiful children; and may G-d grant them health, success, and nachas!

With blessings,

Rabbi Dovid B. Kaplan

Approval from the Biala Rebbe

הובא לפני גליונות בעניני קירוב רחוקים לקרב אחינו בני ישראל אל
אביהם שבשמים, כידוע מהבעש"ט זיע"א שאמר "אימתי קאתי מר
לכשיפוצו מעינותיך חוצה" ואפריון נמטי"ה להאי גברא יקירא מיקירי
צפת עיה"ק תובב"א כמע"כ מוהר"ר משה שטיינרמן שליט"א אשר כבר
עוסק רבות בשנים לקרב רחוקים לתורה וליהדות, וכעת מוציא לאור
ספר בשם "דרכי צדיקים" וראיתי דברים נחמדים מאוד וניכר מתוך
הדברים שהרב בעל המחבר – אהבת השי"ת ואהבת התורה וישראל
בלבבו, ובטחוני כי הספר יביא תועלת גדולה לכל עם ישראל.

ויה"ר שיזכה לבוא לגומרה ברוב פאר והדר ונזכה לגאולתן של ישראל
בב"א.

בכבוד רב:

אהרן שלמה חיים אליעזר
בלאאמו"ר זצ"ל ה' אבי"א

9

Reb Moshe Steinerman

Rabbi M. Lebovits
Grand Rabbi of
Nikolsburg
53 Decatur Avenue
Spring Valley, N.Y. 10977

יוסף יחיאל מיכל
לעבאוויטש
ניקלשבורג
מאנסי - ספרינג וואלי, נ.י.

בעזהשי"ת

בשורותי אלו באתי להעיד על מעשה אומן, מופלא מופלג בהפלגת חכמים ונבונים,
ירא וחרד לדבר ה', ומשתוקק לקרב לבת ישראל לאביהם שבשמים,
ה"ה הרב **משה שטיינערמאן** שליט"א בעיה"ק צפת תובב"א

שעלה בידי להעלות על הספר דברים נפלאים שאסף מספרים הקדושים, בענין אהבה
אחוה שלום וריעות, לראות מעלות הברינו ולא חסרונם, ועי"ז להיות נמנעים מדברי
ריבות ומחלוקת, ולתקן עון שנאת חנם אשר בשביל זה נחרב בית מקדשינו
ותפארתנו, וכמשאחז"ל (ושר. ומהוקא רמה פ״ם ני) על ויחן שם ישראל, שניתנה תורה באופן
שחנו שם כאיש אחד בלב אחד.

וניכר בספר כי עמל זינע הרבה להוציא מתח"י דבר נאה ומתוקן, ע"כ אף תבין
עמו להוציאו לאור עולם, יהי רצון שחפץ ה' בידו יצליח, ויברך ה' חילו ופועל ידו
תרצה, שיברך על המוגמר להנדי"ל תורה ולהאדירה ולהפיצו בקרב ישראל, עד ביאת
גוא"צ בב"א

א"ד הכותב לכבוד התורה ומרביציה,
י"ט חשון תשס"ז

[signature]

Rabbi Abraham Y. S. Friedman
161 Maple Avenue #C Spring Valley NY 10977
Tel: 845-425-5043 Fax: 845-425-8045

רב דביהמ"ד אמר"י ספ"ד קאמאדא
ירושם כולל יצב"י

בעזהשי"ת

ישפות השם החיים והשלו', לכבוד ידידי מאז ומקדם מיקירי קרתא
דירושלים יראה שלם, וזכה ומזכה אחרים, להיות דבוק באלקינו, ה"ה
הר"ר משה שטיינרמאן שליט"א.

שמחתי מאוד לשמוע ממך, מאתר רחוק וקירוב הלבבות, בעסק
תורתך הקדושה ועבודתך בלי לאות, וכה יעזור ה' להלאה ביתר שאת
ויתר עז. והנה שלחת את הספר שלקטת בעניני דביקות בה', לקרב
לבבות בני ישראל לאבינו שבשמים בשפת אנגלית, אבל דא עקא
השפת לא ידענו, ע"כ לא זכיתי לקרותו, ע"כ א"א לי ליתן הסכמה פרטי
על ספרך, ובכלל קיבלתי על עצמי שלא ליתן הסכמות, ובפרט כשאין
לי פנאי לקרות הספר מתחלתו עד סופו, אבל בכלליות זכרתי לך חסד
נעוריך, היאך הי' המתיקות שלך בעבדות השם פה בעירינו, ובנועם
המדות, וחזקה על חבר שאינו מוציא מתחת ידו דבר שאינו מתוקן,
ובפרט שכל מגמתך להרבות כבוד שמים, שבודאי סייעתא דשמיא
ילוך כל ימיך לראות רב נחת מיוצ"ח ומפרי ידיך, שתתקבל הספר
בסבר פנים יפות אצל אחינו בני ישראל שמדברים בשפת האנגלית
שיתקרבו לאבינו שבשמים ולהדבק בו באמת כאות נפשך, ולהרבות
פעלים לתורה ועבודה וקדושה בדביקות עם מדות טובות, בנייחותא
נייחא בעליונים ונייחא בתחתונים עד ביאת גואל צדק בב"א.

כ"ד ידידך השמח בדצלחתך ובעבודתך

אברהם יחזקאל שרגא פרידמאן

שמעון פאלאק

Reb Moshe Steinerman

Table of Contents

Introduction

King Solomon taught us that the beginning of wisdom starts with the fear of *Hashem*. However, how we get to this true fear seems like a long and difficult process. So, there is one shortcut to fear of *Hashem*, love of *Hashem*. The more you love *Hashem*, the more your fear of Him will naturally increase.

A *chassid* wants to attain fear of *Hashem* more than anything in the world, but fear of *Hashem* isn't something you can force. There are things you can do to enhance it, but its main source is within your love of *Hashem*. You must love *Hashem* so much that you fear disappointing Him. Fearing punishment is nice, but it won't do the trick alone. You must use your love and joy of the *mitzvos*, to love Him with all of your heart, to such an extent that you would never purposely sin.

I have chosen to tell stories of piety from our holy sages, rather than the actual teachings they gave over, since they lived as they taught. Seeing their lessons in action is more powerful than just being taught them. I bring before you my favorite stories of holiness, in hopes that these stories bring you to a greater love of *Hashem*, and spiritual yearning.

17

However, conventional methods don't always allow us to express our personal love and affection for the holy One blessed be He. We need to take upon ourselves simple acts of love for Him.

It isn't enough to simply create a fence around us, with hopes of keeping the impurities out. We must also persevere and become dedicated to our devotions. Nothing rises above the simple devotion of *mitzvos*, before *Hashem*. *Hanhagos* cannot replace the beauty of simplicity. What they can do, though, is bring us to an absolute love of our Creator, blessed be He.

My hope is that when you're down, or when you are up, you will read these stories, climbing even higher towards *Hashem*. There is nowhere that He is not. He fills the heavens and the earth. In your very blood, is the *neshamah* that He blessed you with. A soul that is so precious that it is filled with His G-dliness. However, this world can make it difficult to appreciate and connect to the absolute pureness inside of us. Nonetheless, a delightful story can help ignite a spark in a sleeping soul. May it be *Hashem's* will, that through repentance and love of Him, we can draw closer to our essence, remember Him, at all times, and become a true and pure vessel for the *Shechinah,* a second home in Her exile.

Even While I Am Slumbering

The *tzaddik* yearns for *Hashem*, even while sleeping. Rabbi Yechiel was a leading disciple of Rabbi Mordechai of Lechovitz. It was his holy way to sleep two hours and no more. Even while he was sleeping, he always had in his mouth words of longing for *Hashem*. For example, "My soul thirsts for You." Or, "Whenever I speak of Your glory, my heart swoons with Your love." And, "My heart desires You in the night hours," and others like this. He thought of this, all in the middle of his sleep. (Toras Avos, p 284)

Burning With the Fire of *D'vekus*

Once, a *tzaddik* came to visit Rabbi Yisrael of Rizhin, after having been with Rabbi Zusha of Hanipol. Curious, having heard many great things about, the *tzaddik* of Hanipol, the Rizhiner asked him what he had seen there.

He said, "When I entered his room, he was wrapped in a *tallis* and crowned with *tefillin*. I could see that the upper half of his body looked as if burning on fire. It was only after he removed the *tefillin* that he

19

slowly began to take on the appearance of a man of flesh and blood."

Calling Out to *Hashem*

Rabbi Chaim of Tzanz would often pace back and forth in a room, totally absorbed in his holy thoughts and meditations. All the while, he was immersed in loving awareness of the L-rd his G-d, blessed be He. From time to time he would cry out, "There is no place where He is not!" Other times, he would call out, "He fills all worlds and surrounds all worlds!" Sometimes he would call out the Thirteen Articles of Faith. (Mekor Chayim, p. 122, #412)

Four-Part Advice

Everything is seen with its spiritual reality foremost. However, it takes years of purifying one's mind and heart, to attain this.

Rabbi Moshe Vorshiver, of blessed memory, questioned the holy Rabbi Eleazar of Koznitz, "How did you merit becoming a *chassidic rebbe*?" He answered in four parts: "First, I never prayed for myself alone without including others. Second, from everything that I saw I learned a lesson. Third, in everything that I saw, I did not see it physically, but its spiritual essence."

To demonstrate this latter point, he told of how he once traveled with a young scholar to Warsaw. When he went to be with the *chassidim*, the other young man remained behind at the inn. Upon returning there later, he inquired where the young man, his traveling companion, was. They told him, "He's sitting over there." However, to the *rabbi*, he simply appeared to be a goose. He glanced at him more closely and realized that, indeed, it was he. Then he asked him, "What have you been doing?" He responded, "I've been enjoying myself eating – I had a delicious meal of goose."

There was also a fourth thing that the *rabbi* said. He never put his faith, nor trust, in anyone other than *Hashem* alone. (Sifran Shel Tzaddikim p. 68)

Good Work Ethics

The Holy Jew, of Pshischa, shared with his *chassidim* how he learned a lesson from a blacksmith. He said that he merited all of his greatness, and spiritual levels, because of this blacksmith. While a young man, living in his father-in-law's house in Apta, there was a certain blacksmith living close by. The smith worked very hard at his job. Even when it was time to go to sleep, he would still be at work, pounding on his anvil. The Holy Jew said to himself, "If this simple smith works this hard, and for such long hours without allowing himself sleep for the transient things of this world, how can I go to sleep, wasting time that I could be devoting to eternal things?"

It was the same thing during the morning hours, for the smith would arise early from bed, before sunrise, to work. Therefore, the holy Jew could not allow himself to sleep late, for he thought, "If the smith can get up so early just to earn money, how can I sleep?" (Niflaot ha-yehudi, p.59)

A *Mezuzah* Nearby

Rabbi Shneur Zalman of Liadi would always keep a *mezuzah* lying near him to look upon, to remember *Hashem*. He did so in keeping with the verse, "I have placed *Hashem* before me always." He would also often look at the sky [which reminds one of *Hashem*, as in the quote: "The sky resembles the Throne of Glory."] (Beis Rabbi, I, chap. 28, p. 178)

Repeating *Shivisi*

A devout disciple of the Besht, Rabbi Yaakov Koppel Chasid would verbally repeat at all hours of the day, "I have placed *Hashem* before me always." Even during the hours of work and business. (Tiferes Beis Dovid, p. 103)

Never Forget *Hashem*

Rabbi Shneur Zalman of Liadi taught:

You should remember *Hashem*, blessed be He, at all times, as it says, "I have placed the L-rd before me always." The Besht taught, if you forget Him for even a moment consider it a sin, and this will spur you not to forget. Happy is such a person, who does this. (Kisvei Kodesh, p. 24)

One time, the holy Rabbi Meir of Kretchnif, a tzaddik of blessed memory in the world to come, was instructing his children. He said to them, "My children, I can tell you that when I was young, if I ever forgot *Hashem*, blessed be He, for a single minute – I cannot say so for a second, because it is just a second – but I never forgot *Hashem*, for a minute without my whole body being shaken." He went on to explain, "I can tell you that it is all a matter of habit. If you accustom yourself to this, you can converse with someone about everything under the sun, but you will not forget Him for the briefest moment." (Raza d' Vvda, Sh'ar ha-Osiyos, p. 20 #5)

You Will Remember Him

The Holy Jew of Pshischa, of blessed memory, once visited his master, the holy Rabbi of Lublin, of blessed memory, and found him disturbed and sighing deeply. When he inquired why he was sighing so, the *rebbe* told him that he had transgressed the prohibition of "Guard yourself well, lest you forget the L-rd your G-d." For he had forgotten *Hashem* for a moment. The Holy Jew, of blessed memory, took upon himself to comfort his *rebbe* with a *Torah* teaching. The *halacha* states that if a farmer left behind in the field a large measure of grain, an entire *omer*, it was not considered as if he had forgotten it [in which case it could be taken by the poor], even though it did pass from his mind momentarily. For, it is so important to him that he is sure to remember it afterwards. "So too here," he comforted the *rebbe*, "it is not important if you forget *Hashem* momentarily, for you are sure to remember *Hashem* soon." Hearing this, the *rebbe* was relieved. (Seder ha-Yom ha-Katzar, p. 11)

Mastery of One's Limbs

You should keep your eyes closed when you awake [only opening them to gaze on something holy], so that your first sight will be holy things, not the vain things of his world. (Rabbi Yechiel Yehoshua of Biala, Seder ha-Yom, #1)

Already, in his youth, Rabbi Shlomo Leib of Lentshno began to sanctify and purify his limbs and organs [for *Hashem's* service]. He accepted on himself many *hanhagos* of purity and holiness. One of such practices was to make a vow with parts of his body – his mouth, eyes and ears. That they would be faithful to their true purpose and would do nothing against the will of the Holy One, blessed be He.

The *rebbe* shared with the *chassidim* how all the parts of his body assented and joined in the oath, except for his two eyes. His eyes (and our sages, of blessed memory, call eyes the middlemen of sin) were steadfast in their refusal.

One morning the young boy, Rabbi Shlomo Leib, decided that the following day he would not open his eyes, so as not to stumble into transgression by looking at something forbidden. When the day arrived, his mother was astonished to see her son, who always got up early and went to the *beis medrash*, lying in bed with his eyes closed. His mother inquired of him if there was something wrong, but the child did not answer and continued to lie on the bed in silence. Not appreciating his reluctance, his mother, who did not know what this was about, gave him one smack and then another.

Only then did his eyes have mercy on the child, softening their stubborn refusal. They agreed to join in the oath along with the rest of the body and do nothing that would bring harm to the piety of the child, who was holy from birth. (Tiferes Avos, p. 34)

You've Wasted Time in Sleep

We witnessed how our master, teacher and *rabbi*, the holy and pure *rebbe*, Reb Elimelech [of Lizensk], of blessed memory, immediately upon awakening from his sleep would speak to himself in a thunderous voice and say to his soul, "Woe is you, that you've wasted time in sleep!" (Maor v'Shemesh, quoted in Or ha-ner, #1, n)

Simple Fervor for *Hashem*

Once the *rebbe*, Reb Zusha, may his merit protect us, went to see the holy *gaon*, Rabbi Mordechai of Neshkiz, who gave him a room to sleep in. After the stroke of midnight [at which time Reb Zusha rose for *tikkun chatzos* and devotional service until morning] the Elder of Neshkiz overheard how Reb Zusha arose and jumped out of his bed with holy fervor and ran around the room.

After doing this for some time, he called out, "Master of the World, I love You! But what can I do for You? I can't do anything!" Then he ran this way and that as before and repeated the same thing numerous times. Again, and again he did this until eventually he said, "I know what I can do! I can whistle for You!" He started to whistle with such fervor that the Elder of Neshkiz remarked to his comrade, who was standing there with him, "Let's leave here quickly before we get burned up by the breath of his holy mouth." (Ohel Elimelech, p. 134, #341)

Arise, Call Out to *Hashem*

When Rabbi Leibele Eiger of Lublin woke up each morning, he got up from the bed with a great clamor and called out loudly, "I am a servant of the Holy One, blessed be He!" (Gan Hadasim, p. 21)

The *Tallis* of Tears

It is told of Rebbe Nachman of Breslov:

The *rebbe* once presented his old *tallis* to one of his close followers, someone already on a high level. He first remarked to him, "Be careful to treat this *tallis* with respect and honor. You should know that as many threads as there are in this *tallis*, that is how many tears I shed before *Hashem* until I understood what a *tallis* is." (Sichos Haran, quoted in Hishtapchus ha-Nefesh, p. 19)

Winding His *Gartel*

It was the custom of the holy *rabbi*, Rabbi Elimelech of Lizensk, each day after *Mincha*, to talk words of *Torah*, in his sweet way, with his closest disciples. Afterwards, he would go into a special room where he prayed *Ma'ariv* alone, in holiness and purity. One disciple, the holy Rabbi Naftali of Ropshitz, whenever he was with his *rebbe*, always yearned very much to get into that room somehow so he could observe what the *rebbe* was doing there. Once, his curiosity overcame him; he slipped in without anyone knowing it and hid himself under the bed. The holy *rebbe*, may his holy memory be a blessing , went into the room, and closed the door after him.

Reb Naftali observed him girding himself with his *gartel*. When he wrapped it around himself once, the room became filled with a great and wonderful light – something not of this world. When he wrapped it around a second time, the light increased until the Ropshitzer could not bear it any longer and, beginning to faint, he cried out. Rabbi Elimelech heard him, and becoming aware of his presence, remarked, "Naftali, my son, are you here? If you are here when I wind the *gartel* around me the third time, certainly your soul will leave your body from the excess of light. So, depart from here at once." (Ohel Elimelech p. 96, #248)

Every Breath for *Hashem*

Our sages told, "Let every soul praise *Hashem*." (Psalms 150) This means praise Him with every breath. So, you can say, at all times, "Blessed is the Merciful One, King of the Universe, Master of this time," or "of this moment." (Ohr ha-Ganuz l'Tzaddikim p. 45).

Once, the son of a certain *tzaddik* praised his departed father, in the presence of Rabbi Tzvi Hirsh of Ziditchov, saying that he did not cease from his *d'vekus* for even one twentieth, of every twenty-four-hour period. But Rabbi Tzvi Hirsh [who thought this was a small praise for that *tzaddik*] said to him in disappointment, "What are you saying? Young man, I tell you that each, and every, breath that he breathed in was with the name *Elokim*, and every breath he exhaled out with the name *YKVK*, blessed be He and blessed be His name." (Eser Oros, p. 151, #5)

He Ate in My Study

Once, the holy Rabbi Avraham and Rabbi Shneur Zalman were *davening*. When the latter finished first he brought over some food and commenced to eat. Following this incident, Rabbi Avraham refused to study *Torah* with him for three days. Rabbi Shneur

29

Zalman informed Rabbi Avraham's father, the holy *maggid*, about this, and he inquired of his son why he was so angry. Why had he refused to learn with Rabbi Shneur Zalman? Rabbi Avraham explained, "How did he dare to bring something so material [food] into my Garden of Eden!" But under the instruction of his holy father, the *maggid*, he began again to learn with him as before. (Beis Rabbi, I, Chap. 25, page 123, n.2)

Father, Father, He Called out

During *davening*, one of the *chassidim* of the Kotzker Rebbe was crying out to *Hashem*, "Father, Father!" Another *chassid* made a joke of this and called out, "Maybe He's not his Father." [meaning his behavior was not on that spiritual level]. The *rebbe*, upon hearing this, responded to him, "If you cry out often enough, "Father, Father!" He actually becomes your Father in truth." (Siah Sarfei Kodesh, IV, p.29 #8)

Breaking His Heart For *Hashem*

The *goan* and *tzaddik*, Rabbi Levi Yitzchok of Berditchev, of blessed memory, once arose in the morning. To prepare himself for prayer, he meditated on the exaltedness of *Hashem*, blessed be He, and his own lowliness, until he felt that there was no one in the world worse than he – and his heart broke within him. (Derech Tzaddikim, p. 53)

Real Preparation for Prayer

The holy Rabbi Yosef of Neishtadt, once inquired of his master, the Tzanzer Rebbe, "What does the *rebbe* do before prayer?" He answered, "I daven to be able to daven." (Mekor Chayim, p. 111, #372)

My Melodies Purify

A *chassid* once complained to the *tzaddik*, Rabbi Yisrael of Rizhin, about his son-in-law. He said that he wasted his time before the morning prayers, failed to study *Torah* as expected, or go to the *mikvah*, as all the *chassidim* do. The *rebbe* questioned him, "Nevertheless, what does he do then?" The *chassid* responded, "He walks around singing to himself your *nigunim*."

"If so," the *rebbe* said, "you should know that my melodies purify as does the *mikvah*." (Beis Rizhin, p. 120)

The Burning *Maggid*

Of the Maggid of Koznitz it is told:

31

During *davening* he burned like a flaming torch with great fervor, dancing and leaping, and roaring like a lion.

Melting the Hearts of Listeners

Of Rabbi Mordechai of Lechovitz it is told that during prayer, he roared like a lion until the hearts of all who heard him would break and melt like water. (Mazkeret Shem ha-Gedolim, pp. 119-103)

The Energy of His Prayer Service

It is told about the morning prayers of the Koznitzer Maggid that they were a sight to be seen:

During the morning, when the holy *rabbi* arrived at the *shul* to *daven*, he walked through two rows of men. He would be attired in *tallis* and *tefillin*, and was accompanied on both sides by his assistants, who carried large burning candles in their hands. The *maggid* entered with holy emotion and joy, with a *sefer Torah* in his arms. He danced one dance before the holy ark, then he placed the *sefer Torah* therein. Afterwards, he danced again, standing before the stand for the prayer leader. This is where the candelabrum was placed, and they put the candles inside it. That was where he sat, stood, and prayed. During the *Shemoneh Esrey* he often would jump up on his pure table (which was next to the stand) and walked back and forth on it. Following the *Shemoneh Esrey* he danced from the table down to the ground. (Ohalei Shem, p. 30, #9)

He Didn't Feel a Thing

Once, during a war in Russia, a regiment of troops visited the town of Berditchev. As was the custom, they were given a few hours to go through the town pillaging and looting. When some soldiers arrived at the Berditchever synagogue, while the congregation was praying, the *chassidim* fled. However, the *rebbe* was in the middle of *Shemoneh Esrey* and he alone remained, for he heard nothing of what was happening around him.

The soldiers, noticing that he alone was there, began to speak with him, and when he did not answer, they beat him cruelly with a stick, hitting him repeatedly. Upon seeing that it did not affect his concentration even the slightest, they were taken aback. They saw that he did not scream out, nor say a word. They realized that it was not natural for a man of flesh and blood to receive such blows without making a sound. So, they left him, saying, "This is not a man!"

After some time, the *chassidim* returned to the *shul* and found the *rebbe* still there. They finished their prayers, but the Berditchever still said nothing, remaining calm as if nothing had transpired. Upon his return home, he said to his family that he felt some pain in his shoulder. Removing his coat and shirt, they immediately noticed the terrible bruises and wounds. It was clear to everyone that the holy *rabbi* had prayed with such great *d'vekus* that he felt nothing at all. He didn't even have the slightest idea what events had led to the discomfort in his shoulder. (Kulam Ahuvim, p. 30b, Tikkun ha-Nefesh, chap. 15)

Always Repent First

It was told of the great *tzaddik*, Rabbi Menachem of Horodna:

More than all the other prayers and supplications, with which he was accustomed, he could be found continually moving his lips, saying the confession. Before he would pray, especially for a sick person, he would repent with a flood of tears rolling down his cheeks.

Once, a great *Torah* sage asked him about this practice of his. The *tzaddik* responded to him, saying, "I learned this practice from the *Torah* of Moshe, and it is a wonderful way to make your prayers acceptable to *Hashem*, blessed be He. For those people who pray, 'Master of the world, G-d merciful and gracious, patient and full of kindness!', and they make many prayers and supplications, by doing this they arouse from Above the attribute of judgement, to investigate them and their deeds, to see if they are worthy of mercy being shown to them or not. Therefore, what you should do is this: If you want to pray for anything, make a confession at the very beginning, saying, 'I have sinned, etc.' Do this with great humility and with tears in your eyes – and afterward say all your prayers and supplications. Then you will call, and *Hashem* will answer." (Toldos Menachem, p. 103)

Prayer as an Exercise

Of Rabbi Chayim of Tzanz it is spoken:

Once, while he was young, he ran around in his room for several hours, back and forth, with awesome fervor, whispering with his lips moving. Rabbi Shalom of Kaminka went up behind him quietly (Rabbi Chayim, due to his great *d'vekus* did not see the Kaminker Rabbi), and he heard that the holy Tzanzer was repeating over and over, "I mean nothing but You, nothing but You alone." (Mekor Chayim, p. 88, #135)

When Rabbi Yehudah Pesah of Lipsk served *Hashem* during the night hours, his manner of prayer was to run from wall to wall back and forth, bent over as if swimming. He would sing songs and praises of

Hashem, with tears and shouting, with joyful melody and song, all in an astonishing way. Often, this would cause him to wet through his shirt. His personal attendant would then provide him another shirt from the dresser, and there were many times when he went through many shirts in one night. (Shema Shlomo, *II, Yesharaish Yaakov, p. 44, #9)*

My Trip to the Tosher *Rebbe*

I once went to *daven* by the Tosher Rebbe zt"l in Canada, for *Mincha.* I had waited a few days to get inside, for his private prayer, which only allowed for ten *bachurim* to join him in a small room. As usual during the winter, outside it was snowing, and we all were excited to pray with the *rebbe.* As he began, his energy was astounding for a man near 90 years of age. Even though it was well below freezing outside, one of the *chassidim* opened the window and then the *rebbe* surged towards it, *chassidim* jumping out of his way as he went. There was barely any room for us to pray, the room was so small. Yet, there was somehow always room for the *rebbe* to run to the window for air. It felt as if he needed to feel the chilly air in order for his soul not to totally disconnect from his body, the prayers were that intense. His feet, his legs, his arms were all inside the prayers, rocking back and forth as if each limb had a prayer of its own. All I can tell you is that the *rebbe* was as if on fire and we just watched as the flames were moving around the room in

complete attachment to *Hashem*. (Reb Moshe
Steinerman)

From One Side of the Room to the Other

It is told through tradition that Rabbi Akiva
prayed with such tremendous self-abandonment, and
fervor, that he could not remain still. When praying
alone [without a *minyan* – though other people may
have been present] he engaged in so much kneeling
and prostrating that if someone was with him, and
saw him in one corner of the room, when he walked
out and returned moments later, he would find him
in the opposite corner. (Brachos 31)

Hours of *D'vekus*

About Rabbi Meir of Premishlan:

Of his holy ways, we know a few things. When
he prayed, it was with such energy and loudness that
the pillars of the building would shake. As he recited
the *shema* he did so with complete self-sacrifice.
During the morning *davening* on *shabbos*, he would
prostrate himself completely on the floor. He would
lie there in total *d'vekus* for hours on end, until most
of the other worshipers concluded their prayers, and

returned home to eat. Upon finishing their meals, when they returned, they would find him standing and saying the *Shemoneh Esrey* or maybe just finishing the *shema*. (Or ha-Meir, p. 16)

The White Doves

It was said about Rabbi Avigdor Yehudah ha-Levi, the *rabbi* of Koyl:

When he was still a *rabbi* in the city of Bloshky, his holy custom after the morning prayer service was to remain the entire day until nightfall, in the synagogue. He kept the doors locked, in order to keep his practice hidden. All the while, he covered himself in his *tallis* and crowned himself in *tefillin*. It happened once that for one reason, or another, some people looked in through the windows in the women's section, and they saw an amazing sight. The *rabbi* was lying on the floor in *tallis* and *tefillin*, stretched out, arms and legs extended in full prostration before the holy ark, which was open. Encircling his holy body were many white doves, while he poured out his heart in prayer before his Creator, blessed be He. (Abir-ha-Ro'im, #141)

An Angel of *Hashem*

It is said of Rabbi Menachem Mendel of Kossov that:

His holy way was to lead the congregation in prayer himself, instead of allowing someone else this holy task. In the synagogue there was a screen, between him and the people, who would hear his clear and sweet voice. They too would direct their hearts to pray. They did so with love and fear of *Hashem*, in a sweet way. No one would ever dare to look over the screen, into the holy place, during the time of prayer.

However, once someone lifted himself up on the wall of the screen to look over, and was startled and jumped back, falling on the ground. He lay there like a stone, and only with difficulty did they bring him back to consciousness. Upon regaining his consciousness, he related how he saw the holy *rabbi* fully prostate on the ground and a fire was blazing all around him as if he were an angel of *Hashem*. That was why when he looked he was stricken and fainted. (Even Shtiya, p. 22, #1)

Not a Service of the Head

A *chassid* once came to Rabbi Simcha Bunim, of Pshischa, and related the troubles he was having. Whenever he prayed, he always got a headache from his concentration. "What has prayer to do with the head?" the *rebbe* answered in surprise. "Prayer is service of the heart, not a labor of the head." (Midor Dor, vol. 1, p. 212)

Strength for *Mitzvos*

Rabbi Yisrael, of Koznitz, was in poor health from his childhood through adulthood. He was always in a bed, since he was so sick and frail. However, when he prayed he would burn with love of *Hashem* like a flaming fire. He was so thin that the doctors were amazed how he could remain alive, for his thighs had no flesh on them at all. His legs were as thin as those of a deer. So weak was he that they had to carry him around to bring him to the *shul*. However, when they brought him to the door of the synagogue he called out in a thunderous voice, "How full of awe is this place!" He then put his feet on the ground, and almost flew to the prayer-leader's stand. Why? Because *Hashem* gives strength to perform his commandments! A strength which is not even human. (Eser Oros, p. 69, #10)

Amen, With Thunder

In the city of Plunsk, the elderly men would tell over tales of the tremendous, holy service of prayer, they saw in the Tzanzer Rebbe, when he used to live there. They related that when he said, "*Amen,* may His great Name..." his voice was a roar and like a thunderclap in a storm, with awesome holiness. (Mekor Chayim, p. 142, #87)

The Spiritual Thoughts During Business Hours

Rabbi Yisrael, of Salant, was once sitting among his close followers. He was discussing with them the ways of life and speaking words of *mussar*. They began to ponder the question of who is higher. Someone who sits in the *beis medrash*, turning his nights into days while occupying himself with *Torah* study, prayer and other Divine service, or someone who sits in his store and conducts his business dealings with faithfulness to the *Torah*'s teachings? "It is known," told Rabbi Yisrael, "that there is nothing higher than doing business in faithfulness. But, that being so, how sad it is when someone who is occupied in business spends his time thinking he should have his attention on kerosene, salt, or the salted fish [rather than the spiritual tasks involved]!" (*Midor Dor*, vol 2, #1366)

Work is a Way to Bestow Kindness Towards Others

Once, Rabbi Yitzchok was traveling with the holy *rabbi*, Reb Dovid'l of Lelov, of blessed memory, and they arrived at the town of Elikish at 1 a.m. The *rebbe*, Reb Dovid'l, did not wish to wake anyone, to ask for a place to sleep. His love for all Jews was so great that he did not want to wake anyone for his own benefit. "So," the Vorker told, "we went to Reb Berish's bakery [for he would be awake and at work]. When we reached there, we found him at work, by the oven, and Reb Berish [who was a devout *chassid* and disciple of Rabbi Dovid] was embarrassed at being found this way, engrossed in such lowly manual labor. However, in all sweetness, the holy Lelover said to him, 'Oh, if only *Hashem* would let me earn my living by the work of my hands! For the truth is that every man of Israel in his innermost heart, which even he doesn't know, wants to do something good for his fellow man. So, everyone who works – as a shoemaker, tailor, baker, or who serves others needs for money – on the inside he doesn't do this work to make money, but rather to do good to his fellow man – even though he does receive money for his trouble. However, this is secondary and unimportant, because it is obvious that he must accept money, in order to live. Nonetheless, the inner meaning of his work is that he wants to show kindness to his fellow man.'"

Rabbi Yitzchok of Vorki taught, "From the words of Reb Dovid'l we can understand that everyone who works to serve others is fulfilling the *mitzvah* of showing kindness, even if his intention is just to receive money in return for his work." (GMvGhTz, Chelek 2, p. 14)

Always Be First

Chazal teach us, "Receive everyone warmly and with joy." (Avos 1:15, 3:16) Also, "Always be first in greeting all men with the blessing of peace." (Avos 4:22)

It was said of Rabbi Yochanan ben Zakkai that no one had ever greeted him with the blessing of peace before he had himself greeted the other first – not even a *goy* in the marketplace. (Brachos 17)

The Warmth of Greeting Everyone

Rabbi Arye Levin once explained: "I was very careful to receive everyone cheerfully, until this became second nature to me. I was careful, to take the initiative in greeting everyone." (A Tzaddik in Our Time, p. 464)

Holiness Preparing Meals

Rabbi Levi Yitzchok of Berditchev told how Queen Esther made a meal with such holiness, and purity, that *kedusha* rested on each, and every dish of food. Even upon the table and all its utensils. (Ohalei Shem, p. 26, #45)

Serving Another Sage

Placing food upon the table is a great service of *Hashem*; even more so is removing the dishes from the table after the meal. (Rabbi Asher of Stolin, Beis Aharon, p. 286)

The Baal Shem Tov once traveled to be with Rabbi Yitzchok, of Drobitch, may his merit protect us, to offer him personal service. It is known that it is a great act of devotion to *Hashem*, and purifies the soul, to offer personal service to one of the holy sages. So, the Besht himself brought to Rabbi Yitzchok his coffee in a pot and served him. When he was finished drinking, the Besht removed the pot, the cup and spoon from the table, bringing them into the kitchen. Rabbi Yitzchok's son, the holy Rabbi Yechiel Michal of Zlotchov replied to the Besht, "Holy *rabbi*, I can understand why you want to offer personal service to my holy father, but I don't understand why you also troubled yourself to carry out the empty dishes?" The Besht answered him by explaining that carrying the spoon out from the Holy of Holies [in the Temple] was also part of the service of the high priest on the Day of Atonement. (Mishnas Chassidim, p. 420, #21)

Measure Your Food

Rabbi Avraham of Slonim shared his private *avodah* during his youth:

When I was a boy of eight I used to eat because I was hungry, but my father would rebuke me saying, "Why are you stuffing yourself?" I didn't know what he wanted from me. But later, when I had grown up a bit, I understood what he meant. So, I made myself a "fence". I decided before a meal how much to eat because once you start eating, and your stomach expands, you can be dragged into overeating. (Toras Avos, Maasei Avos, #167)

Connecting While at Work

Chanoch was a shoemaker who would sew together the upper and lowers of the shoes. (*Bereshis* 5:24) With every stitch he would remark, "Blessed is His glorious kingdom forever and ever!" He was able to bind together the upper and lower Worlds. (HeDvat Simha, p. 57)

Looking at the Holy Name During the Meal

During their first meeting, Rabbi Yitzchak, of Drobitch, and the Baal Shem Tov ate the *shabbos* meal together, at the Besht's house on *shabbos*. At the table, directly after the *kiddush*, our master and *rabbi*, Rabbi Yitzchak, placed before himself a small silver plate on which the name YKVK was engraved. He rested it against his thumb. For it was his holy practice to have this little plate before him while he ate, and whenever he took food into his mouth he looked at the Name. He did this throughout the whole course of the meal. (Mazkeret Shem ha-Gedolim, p. 4)

Concentration While Eating

During his journey, to the Besht, Rabbi Yitzchak was served some bread at an inn, and as always he glanced at the name of *Hashem* on the silver plate, while eating. When he was done with the bread he was served, he asked for some more.

The female innkeeper returned with more bread, and seeing that he was hungry, continued giving him more each time he ate what was placed before him. The entire time, he was continuously looking at the name of *Hashem*. Eventually, he had eaten so much she had nothing remaining to give him. After some time, the holy Rabbi Yitzchak lifted his head slowly, as if waking up, and inquired of her where was the bread he had ordered. It seems that he was so immersed in his holy meditations of the name of *Hashem*, engraved on the plate, that he was not at all aware that he had already eaten so much more bread than what he had originally requested. (Raza d'Uvda, Sh'ar ha-osiyos, p. 25, #2)

Not to Bend Down While Eating

Rabbi Yechiel Michal, of Zlotchov, said that it was his practice to never bend down to the food, but rather to sit upright, and bring the food to his mouth. (Mazkeres Shem ha-Gedolim, p. 26)

This was so that he should not be drawn into the physical lust that bending over could lead to. For, someone who has a strong desire to eat, bends down to the plate. (ibid. p.55)

In a comparable manner, Rabbi Yisrael of Rizhin, never moved his mouth toward the utensil with which he ate. (Beis Rizhin, p. 232)

Don't Give Into Lust

Our teacher and *rabbi*, Rabbi Yitzchok of Neshkiz, told how when he was a child he sat at the table with his father, Rabbi Mordechai. He had wanted to drink some water after eating some fish, but his father instructed him to wait a little. However, when his father turned away, he took the water and drank. Having caught him in the act, his father reproached him sternly and said, "Now you are little, and you lust for this. What will happen when you grow up and lust for something else?" The *rabbi* recalled, "I began to cry, and I cried and cried. But I

47

put those words on my heart, so, as to remember them always. Since then they have always been in my heart and I've never forgotten them." (Mazkeres Shem ha-Gedolim, p. 100)

A Holy Phone Message

"I once wanted to make a phone call to a *tzaddik* in the USA. I donned my coat, hat, and a *gartel* just to phone him. Sometimes I even run to the *mikvah* first before calling. So, this time, you know what happened? After all my preparations, I reached the *tzaddik*'s answering machine. Wow, so at least I left a message in holiness, no?" (Reb Moshe Steinerman)

Holy Father, Holy Father

The Maggid of Mezritch taught, a man should call out to the Holy One, blessed be He, saying, "Father!" until He becomes his father. (Eser Oros, p. 28, #21)

It was a practice of Rabbi Dovid Moshe of Tchortkov, while sitting at his pure table before *Hashem* together with his disciples, to call out again and again, "Holy Father! Holy Master of the World!" (Eser Oros, p. 147, #8)

Torah Before Eating

Rabbi Yaakov Yosef of Polnoye, a principal disciple of the Baal Shem Tov, would study seven pages of *Talmud* before eating. Even during his meal, between dishes, he did not stop reciting his studies. (In Praise of the Baal Shem Tov, #52)

Study Sessions While Eating

We hear of Rabbi Yaakov Yehudah of Nadzrin (the son-in-law of Rabbi Menachem Mendel of Vorki) that, while eating his meal, he would learn *Torah*. Not only this though, during the meal, he had many different study-sessions set for himself in different areas of *Torah*. (Ha-Tzaddik ha-Shotek, p. 126)

Strange Movements

It was once said that the holy Rabbi Shmelke of Nikolsburg made strange movements while praying, and the holy Rabbi Levi Yitzchok of Berditchev, makes even stranger ones when eating. (Zichron l'Rishonim, p. 95)

Food as a Sacrifice

One day, three *tzaddikim* came together at the house of the holy *Maggid*. They were Rabbi Yisrael of Koznitz (the Holy Jew of Pshischa), Reb Fishel of Strikov, and Reb Dovid of Lelov. The *Maggid* received them all warmly and joyfully, as was his custom. He even gave orders as to where each of them would sit with him at the table. The Holy Jew was given a place right next to the *Maggid*, so they could talk. There they conversed in a very intimate and spiritual way about *Torah*. Reb Fishel very much wished to listen to what they were saying, so he bent over to pick up on their conversation. Meanwhile, Reb Dovid'l was occupied in eating his bread and butter.

The *Maggid* then turned to the Reb Fishel, and pointed to the Reb Dovid'l saying, "Why don't you learn from this young man who knows what to do? He eats one piece of bread spread with butter and offers a sacrifice in eating it. He eats another piece of buttered bread – another sacrifice." (P'ri Kodesh Chillulim, p. 18)

D'vekus While Eating

It is told of the holy Rabbi Arye Leib Lipshitz, of Vishnitz:

He never ate except while at a *mitzvah* meal
[such as a *shabbos* meal or a feast celebrating a *bris*].
One time the holy *rabbi*, our teacher Rabbi Meir, the
son of the *tzaddik* Rabbi Eleazar of Dzikov, of blessed
memory, came to him and remained with him for
shabbos. When he arrived home after *shabbos*, his father
asked him, "What did you see while you were visiting
the holy *gaon*?" His son answered, "Father, I saw that
he didn't eat soup with a spoon, but with a fork, due
to his *d'vekus*. His *d'vekus* was so intense that he didn't
realize." (Dor Deah, vol. 1,)

A similar story is told about Rabbi Leibele
Eiger, of Lublin:

Once during the third meal on *shabbos*, when he
made *hamotzi* on his bread, he cut his finger. Although
others would easily feel the pain, due to his great
concentration, he was unaware of his injury. The
blood continued flowing until others at the table saw
it, and came to his aid. (Gan Hadasim, p. 21)

A Meal Through the Morning

About Reb Chaim of Tzanz it was told:

One time, during the evening meal of the holy
shabbos, the dessert was brought to the table, but the
rebbe, as was his custom, was immersed deeply in

51

d'vekus. This time it continued for an extraordinary number of hours throughout the night. By the time he returned to normal consciousness, the day had already dawned. The *rebbe* then called out, "The sun has come up, but for the honor of the holy *shabbos* we'll rely on the opinion of the holy Belzer Rebbe that it's still considered night [and we are permitted to finish the meal]!" (Rabbeinu ha-Kodesh mi-Tzanz, p. 80)

Once, on the evening of the holy *shabbos*, Rabbi Nachman of Breslov and his followers washed their hands before the meal and made a blessing over the bread. Then they all ate the piece of bread over which they had made the blessing. However, as soon as Rabbi Nachman ate his piece, his mind ascended, and he cleaved to *Hashem*, blessed be He, with great *d'vekus.* With tremendous awe, he just remained in one place silently, his eyes open, in a powerful and wondrous *d'vekus* the entire night. No one else at the table dared to put out a hand to eat any of the food that was on the table, for they were completely astonished at his state, and feared that they would disturb him. Finally, dawn came, and the first rays of the sun appeared. They all recited the Grace after Meals, left the table [without eating more than the one bite of bread] and went home. (Shivchei Moharan, p. 7)

We Still Need You

Once when Rabbi Naftali of Ropshitz was with his master, Reb Elimelech of Lizensk during the third *shabbos* meal, it occurred to him that Reb Elimelech was so high in *d'vekus* that he was close to removing his soul from his body altogether. Fearing that *Hashem* forbid he could leave this world, he quickly began to pound on the table to disturb him and bring him down. When the *rebbe* complained to him afterwards and questioned how he dared to disturb his *d'vekus*, the Ropshitzer defended his actions. "Holy master," he said, "we will need you in this world." (Ohel Nafali, p.45, #125)

Full Concentration During *Benching*

It is well known how our master, Rabbi Dov Ber [the Maggid of Mezritch], may his merit protect us, taught the importance of full intention when reciting the Grace after Meals. This should be even more so than during the daily prayer services. (Hanhagos Tzaddikim III, vol. 2, p. 748)

Awaiting Expectantly For the Moment

Rabbi Levi Yitzchok of Berditchev was famous for the fervor with which he performed the *mitzvos*.

53

His Divine service in doing the commandments of *Hashem* was with the most powerful love, and the most intense longing, as if a fire was burning in his bones.

The night following *yom tov* he could not sleep. He had such a longing to put on *tefillin* the next morning [*tefillin* are not used on *yom tov*] that he remained awake the whole night in expectation. He anxiously was looking for the dawn to come so he could don the holy *tefillin*.

During the first night of *Succos* he also would stay awake the entire night waiting for the moment that the first light would arrive, so that he could fulfill the *mitzvah* of the four species [*esrog, lulav, aravos,* and *hadassim*]. When the time did finally arrive, he took them in his hands, his joy knew no bounds, as if he had just found the greatest treasure. He would kiss them with all his heart, and with the greatest love.

That was his way, with all objects used for any of the *mitzvos*. He would appreciate them, and kiss them, with all his heart. Not only this, but when he performed any *mitzvah*, all of his limbs would be on fire, in the most wondrous and awesome *d'vekus*, so that he was entirely separated from this world. (Toldos Kedushas Levi, p. 16)

Dancing On the Eve of *Shabbos*

About Rabbi Nissan Chayim of Brodshin it is told that his *d'vekus* on *shabbos* was out of this world. Following his meal, he would always dance in honor of *Hashem*. Following his dancing [on *shabbos* evening after the meal] his *payos* and beard would be dripping with sweat. This was all from the greatness of his service of *Hashem* in dancing, and the holiness of *shabbos* that burned within him. This happened even though he did not dance with exertion, but rather softly and quickly. The fire that burned within him brought out much water [*mayim rabbim*], as if he had just stepped out of the *mikvah*. (Toldos Rabbi Nissan Chayim mi-Brodshin, Raza d'Uvda, p. 144)

Sweating the Fear of *Hashem*

One of the *chassidim* of Rabbi Shalom Yosef [a son of the Rizhiner] was near the *rebbe's* room while he was praying. Though he was standing close to the door, he did not hear any sound of the *rebbe's* voice, nor any movements from his prayer. All he could hear was the soft tread of his feet, as he paced about the room. After a few hours, the *rebbe's* attendant went inside. When he came out he had in his hand the *rebbe's* shirt. It was soaking wet. The *chassid* was astonished at this sight, since the *rebbe* was in no way exhausting himself physically. He became even more astonished when the attendant told him that this happened every day.

This *chassid* also would spend time with the *tzaddik*, Arye Leibush, the head of the religious court of Tomashov. At the first opportunity, he related to the *rabbi*, with great excitement, what he had seen and heard. The *rabbi* of Tomashov said to him, "This is the level mentioned in *Kedushas Keter,*" [the prayer] of *Rosh Hashanah*: "Sweating without cease from fear of the Throne [of *Hashem*]." (Bais Rizhin, p. 287)

For the Sake of the Unification

Rabbi Yitzchok Issac of Komarna said about his *rebbe*, Rabbi Tzvi Hirsh of Ziditchov:

"I saw how my teacher, my holy uncle, our master Rabbi Tzvi Hirsh, used to say out loud before every task that he performed, 'For the sake of the unification of the Holy One, blessed be He, and His *Shechinah.*' – even when he drank a little water." (Ateres Tiferes, p. 7, #27)

Keep Running

The way of the holy Rabbi Dovid of Amshinov, was to always walk quickly as if almost running. This is because he was always either running to do a *mitzvah* or running away from transgression. (Siah Srfei Kodesh, II, p. 121, #467)

Satisfaction to *Hashem*

The holy Seer of Lublin had a firm practice from his youth that he would not think, speak, or do anything, except for what gave satisfaction or pleasure to *Hashem*. (Seder ha-Yom ha-Katzar, p. 12)

The Illusionary Woman

The Rebbe of Lublin, when he was a young man, once went to be with his master the holy *rabbi*, Reb Elimelech of Lizhenzsk, of blessed memory. Once as he traveled along, there was a downpour of heavy rain and extreme cold. The way became foggy and he eventually lost his way while trekking through the thick forest. Some time went by, and he eventually came upon a house with lit windows. He went there and entered. It was very warm and pleasant inside. He felt relieved and much better after having suffered so much from the rain and the cold.

Inside one of the rooms there was only a single woman who was young and pretty. Still needing to warm up, the *rebbe* did not know what to do about the prohibition of being alone with a woman. After a few moments inside, it became clear she wanted to talk

57

him into sinning. She began telling him she was unmarried and ritually clean. The *rebbe* became very distressed by her enticements, and her attempted seduction. Even though he felt he was losing his strength of resistance, he at last remembered the fence he had made for himself and answered her, saying, "I have accepted on myself not to do anything, even something permitted, except what gives pleasure to my Creator. I don't see what satisfaction *Hashem* will derive from this?"

As soon as he finished uttering these words he saw that the whole scene before him was imaginary – there was no forest, no house, and no woman. They were all illusions, simply to test him. Seconds later he found himself alone, by the side of the road, on the path he had to go on. (Eser Oros, p. 89, #23)

Carrying a Gift for the King

There was a simple man, who was bringing a gift to the king. However, he was afraid of the highwaymen he might meet while embarking on the road, for they were known to hide in wait for travelers. So, he came up with a plan in order to feel comfortable and safe during his journey. As he went along, for the entire length of his journey, he cried out loudly that he was carrying a gift to the king. His thoughts were that this way the highwaymen would be afraid to bother him, for anyone who dared harass someone carrying something of the king's was sure to meet a dire fate at the hands of the army.

When you are engaged in doing a holy deed, for then the forces of the other side are always ready to snatch and steal what you are doing, trying to bring it under its power [by leading you into wrong motives]. However, if you say, "I am doing this for the sake of the unification of the Holy One, blessed be He, and His *Shechinah*. I am carrying a gift to the King of the Universe." – who will dare to steal what belongs to the King? (Zichron l'Rishonim, p 38, n. 26)

What You Hear, is a Message for You.

Once during *Rosh Chodesh Elul* [which leads into *Rosh Hashanah* and *Yom Kippur*] the *rabbi* and *tzaddik* Rabbi Levi Yitzchok of Berditchev was standing in his house, looking out the window at the street. A shoe repairman passed along and asked him, "Don't you have something to fix?" Immediately the *tzaddik* sat down on the floor wailing and crying, "Woe is me, and alas for my soul! For the day of judgement is fast approaching and I still haven't fixed myself!" (Zichron l'Rishonim, p. 96)

A Message from *Hashem*

The holy Rabbi Simcha Bunim of Pshischa was a merchant before he became famous as a *rebbe*. One time, he went to the market to purchase produce, and he wanted to buy what a particular farmer was selling. The farmer wanted more money than he was willing to offer. The farmer remarked to the holy *rabbi* in Polish, "Do better" – meaning that he should make a better offer on the price. However, a *tzaddik* takes words to heart as a message to him from *Hashem*. So, when Rabbi Bunim returned home, he thought that if even the farmer was trying to arouse him to better, the time had come that he should do *teshuva*. (Siah Sarfei Kodesh, I, p. 33, #160)

Intensive Prayer and Torah

We are told that Rabbi Zusha of Hanipoli would pray the morning service until noon, calling out with cries so awesome that they were beyond human nature. After praying, he learned *Torah* with the same amazing intensity as in his prayer. (Mazkeres Shem ha-Gedolim, p. 64)

Holy Tears

When Rabbi Meir of Kretchnif learned *gemara*, tears flowed from his eyes without cease. It would continue, until the book he was learning from would be wet and waterlogged from the tears that fell down from his holy eyes. (Raza d'Uvda, p. 4)

Gemara in Simplicity

I heard, about a simple man, who studied *gemara* without understanding what the words meant. His practice was just to recite the words in simplicity, yet through this he reached the level where he had mystical revelations of Eliyahu Hanavi. (Derech Tzaddikim, p. 49, #10)

Teshuva Before Torah Study

Rabbi Eleazar Mendel, of Jerusalem, hired a private *Torah* teacher for his young son. He was astounded when his son told him, how during every day before he was taught, his teacher would stand completely still at the window staring out into space. His eyes would stream tears, like rainwater. That same day, the *rebbe* called the teacher to his house, and compelled him to explain his strange behavior.

The teacher agreed to share his story. Many years earlier, he had seen a miracle, a revelation of *ruach hakodesh*, by the Holy Grandfather of Radoshitz. One night, his curiosity overcame him, and he wanted to witness the *rebbe's* private observances to *Hashem*. Excited, that very night he hid in the *rebbe's* room, to

61

see what his devotions were in the hours when others slept. Early on he was discovered, however, and started to run away in great fear.

The *rebbe* stopped him and asked, "Young man, what were you seeking?"

"The fear of heaven!" the young man responded. "May it be His will," remarked the *rebbe*, 'that whenever you begin to learn *Torah*, thoughts of *teshuva* sparkle within you!"

"This is what the *rebbe* blessed me with," said the teacher. "Since then, tens of years have already passed, but the *rebbe*'s blessing is still in force, and a day never passes that I don't do *teshuva*. From the moment I get ready to learn *Torah*, feelings of *teshuva* are awakened in my heart and my eyes stream with tears." (Tiferes Beis Dovid, p.18)

Arise and Study Torah Standing

It is told that the Kotzker Rebbe, in his younger days, was a *misnagid* and against the *chassidim*. He was so assiduous in continual *Torah* study that he learned while standing up the entire day, holding in his hands a large, heavy copy of the Amsterdam edition of the *Talmud*, with its wooden covers and heavy clasps of burnished brass. (Shivihei Tzaddikim, p 42)

Learning while Standing

It is told of Rabbi Zusha of Hanipoli:

It was his holy way, that after praying the evening service, he would study *Torah* all night, while standing. Not only this, but he also slept only two hours. (Mazkeres Shem ha-Gedolim, p. 64)

The Fragrance of the Garden of Eden

Our holy master, the Rabbi of Lublin, said that while studying in the *yeshiva* of the holy *gaon*, Rabbi Shmelke of Nikolsburg, he would smell the fragrance of the Garden of Eden while he learned from the *rebbe*. However, the *rebbe* would try his best to hide this. For whenever he learned with the talmidim he had on the table many kinds of spices, so that if one of them would detect something he would think it was just the spices. (Ohel Elimelech, p. 135, #343)

The Parchment of the Baal Shem Tov

A *chassid* once inherited a special card from his ancestors, and he wished to bestow it as a gift to the Seer of Lublin. He embarked on a trip to see the holy master. As he went, he carried in his hand two pieces of parchment. On one, which he had made, there was written [in Hebrew], "I have placed the L-rd before me always." He used to hold this card in front of him whenever he learned *Torah*. The other card was from the Baal Shem Tov himself, in his own handwriting. It had the four-letter name of *Hashem*. This card had been given as a present to the *rabbi's* father, who had been a disciple of the Besht.

When he came before the Lubliner and showed him the first card which he had written, the Seer gazed at it carefully and remarked, "Ah! Light! Light!" Then the *rabbi* showed him the second card from the Baal Shem Tov, with its black letters on the white parchment. Immediately, the *rebbe* leaped up from his chair and called out with emotion, "Black fire on white fire!" So ecstatic was he, when he saw the holy writing. With an expression of deep gratitude, he eagerly took from himself these precious and invaluable gifts, cherishing them. (Kol Sippurei Baal Shem Tov, vol. 1, p. 242, story)

The Master of the Book is Teaching You

Rabbi Simcha Bunim of Pshischa once related this story to his *talmidim*: Once he came to his *rebbe* The Holy Jew, of blessed memory. His *rebbe* was surprised to see how terribly depressed he appeared. He asked him what had happened and the reason for his sadness. Rabbi Simcha Bunim told him that someone had just humiliated him in the worst way, so that he was deeply hurt inside. His *rebbe* was surprised, and asked who would dare to do this, but Rabbi Simcha Bunim wouldn't tell him. He urged him to tell because he wanted to punish whomever it was. When he continued in his refusal, the *rebbe* became angry. He inquired of Rabbi Simcha what he answered back after he was humiliated. He told him that he kissed the one who did it, on the mouth. At this the *rebbe* was astonished and finally ordered him, as his *rebbe*, to tell him who it was.

'So, having no choice, I was forced to tell him. I said to him that in the Jerusalem *Talmud* (Shabbos, perek 1, halacha 32) it says that when you are learning you should consider the master of the tradition as if he were standing before you. That was my thought while I was studying the book of character development, Shevas Musar. So, the holy author was shaming and humiliating me greatly, until I saw that I hadn't even begun to serve *Hashem*, and that I hadn't the slightest bit of the fear of *Hashem* or holy shame or any one of the many virtues that a son of Avraham, Yitzchok, or Yaakov should have. When I saw that what he said was all true I was overcome with shame and almost fainted. But afterwards, I took the holy book in my hands, kissed it with all my heart, and then placed it back on the bookcase along with all the other books."

When the Holy Jew heard his disciple "explain" what had happened to him he became very happy and joyful at his wisdom. [This truly is how a *chassid* should learn *Torah*.] (Simchas Yisrael p. 27, #65)

The Wisdom of a Melody

When Rabbi Shneur Zalman, of Liadi was in Shklov, he was asked by the *Torah* scholars many questions, before he went to give a *shiur* in the *beis medrash*. When he arose to the *bimah*, he said, "Instead of speaking words of *Torah,* and answering your questions, I will sing a melody for you. This is because souls are elevated and brought to *Hashem* by means of melody and song." He then began to sing with lofty *d'vekus*. A hush descended upon the *beis medrash,* and the room was filled with complete silence, all becoming deeply immersed in thought. Unexpectedly, in the middle of the *rebbe's nigun,* the *Torah* sages of Shklov felt that all their questions and difficulties were resolved. The *rebbe,* with his use of melody, a *nigun* of *d'vekus,* had opened for them channels from the foundations of wisdom. Their minds became open and all their thoughts became clear. One of them remarked afterwards, "When my question was answered, I felt as if I was a small child." (Sippurei Chassidim, vol 1, #446)

The Psalm Sayer

Another story, in which the Besht appears, speaks of the greatness of a simple and righteous man. He was called by the people of his town, "the Psalm sayer." This is because the Book of Psalms was always heard coming from his mouth. He was accustomed to saying psalms from memory, during whatever work he was doing. (Kol Sippurei Baal Shem Tov, II, Chap. 13, story 14)

Maggid From Heaven

The Rebbe of Lubin first lived in the city of Lanzhut, in the province of Galitzia. He recalled that there lived a simple man, who through the power of his recitation of psalms, with great and pure *kavanah*, merited having an angelic preacher from Heaven. This being would appear to him from time to time and teach him *Torah*. (Hisgalus ha-Tzaddikim, p. 21)

Reciting the Psalms

As a boy, Rebbe Nachman of Breslov recited numerous psalms. His father's house had a small garret, partitioned off as a storehouse for hay and feed. It was here that future *rebbe* would hide himself, chanting the psalms, and begged *Hashem* that he be worthy of drawing close to Him. He also had the practice of chanting only the verses in the psalms speaking of prayer and the cry to *Hashem*. Often, he would go through the entire book of psalms in one stretch, saying only those verses and leaving out the rest. (Shevachay HaRan, #10)

Uprooting Trees with Prayer

A story is told of how Rabbi Yaakov Yosef of Polnoye used the psalms as a *tikkun* to repair a sin of speech. One time, he unfortunately said an unnecessary blessing, and he was very distraught, as it is forbidden to utter without purpose. Thereafter, he had a dream in which he was shown that, as a result of his transgression, he had planted, so to speak, a garden of trees in the realm of uncleanness. To repair his sin, and to uproot those trees, he did the following:

He grabbed the Book of Psalms in his hand and said in a thunderous voice the first book [of the five], and at the sound of his sincere prayer, the whole heavenly host trembled. One of the angels came to him and said, "Know that the fruits of the trees have fallen off." He said the second Book of Psalms with a loud voice, and another angel appeared to him and said, "Know that the leaves have fallen off." Then he said the third book, and one came and said, "The small branches have fallen off." He said the fourth book in a loud voice and was told, "The big branches have fallen off." Finally, he said the fifth book and an angel appeared, saying, "Know that the trees themselves have fallen." (L'Yesharim Tehillah, p. 10)

A Vessel for the World of Thought

When you are sitting alone in silence, you should imagine that you are a vessel for the world of thought, for you draw this on yourself. As soon as you come out of meditation, however, and go from stillness to movement, see that everything be done as a unification, joining your movement, speech, and walking [all together as one, in *Hashem* G-d consciousness], that they all be done in holiness, just as your thought was sanctified when you were meditating. You should also move, speak and walk so as to receive the yoke of the Kingdom of Heaven, which keeps you in existence from nothingness, and so as to do the will of the Kingdom of Heaven – and by this you accomplish a unification. (Or ha-Ganuz l'Tzaddikim p. 46)

No Trouble Allowed on *Shabbos*

Rabbi Moshe of Koznitz once overheard a *chassid* sigh during *shabbos*. He said to him, "Even sighing and being troubled over spiritual things is forbidden on *shabbos*." (Derech Emunah u'Maaseh Rav, p.91)

The Bounty Depends on Speech

Once, on *erev shabbos*, as the holy *shabbos* drew near, in the house of Rabbi Menachem Mendel of Rimanov there was still no fish [as traditional] in honor of the holy *shabbos*. However, the *rebbe* seemed undisturbed, and he even instructed his holy servant, Rabbi Tzvi Hirsh, to put a number of empty frying pans on the fire on the stove. Making sure that each time he did so he was to say, "In honor of the holy *shabbos*."

Rabbi Tzvi Hirsh did as he was instructed. While he was thus engaged, someone came from afar to visit the *rebbe*, and as a gift, he brought with him some fish in honor of the holy *shabbos*. Everyone in the household was astonished when this happened.

On the day of the holy *shabbos* the *rebbe* explained to them, "When the holiness of the *shabbos* descends from Heaven there comes with it a flow of supernal beneficence. Someone, who wants to receive this supernal flow of goodness, must bring his desire to do so into speech, and to say with complete devotion, 'In honor of the holy *shabbos*.' Then, what will transpire, is that the flow will come down of itself from Above, for the bounty depends on speech. So, do not be amazed that I was so sure there would be fish in honor of the holy *shabbos*." (Ateres Menachem, p. 19, #46)

A Rare Vision of Light

Rabbi Zev Wolf of Zhitomir told:

Once on Friday the great Maggid of Mezritch sat in his room, which was adjacent to his *beis medrash*. He recited the *Torah* portion of the week, twice *Torah* /once *Targum*. A few of his students were sitting in the *beis medrash* studying when abruptly a great light shone on them. Instantly, the door of the *Maggid's* room opened and his flaming countenance was revealed to their eyes. This rare vision of him almost caused them to lose their minds. Usually, he kept his full holiness more hidden. Rabbi Pinchas of Frankfort, his brother Rabbi Shmelke of Nikolsburg, Rabbi Elimelech of Lizhenzsk and his brother Rabbi Zusha of Hanipol, all fled outside.

Rabbi Levi Yitzchok of Berditchev reacted differently. He went into a state of total ecstasy and rolled on the floor under the table. Even he, who was so unused to any emotionalism, clapped his hands in uncontrollable excitement. (Ha-Maggid mi-Mezritch, p. 69)

Forgiveness Before Accepting *Shabbos*

"I was once asking my fellow Jews for forgiveness, and they began to rebuke me for the lack of positivity I was showing thereby. I then told them, this proves my point, I need to ask forgiveness for not teaching *chassidus* better, so you would have understood what I meant." So, I began telling the following story to them and at the end, they understood. (Reb Moshe Steinerman)

This was heard it from our master, teacher and *rabbi*, the Rabbi of Berniv. Once a holy sage traveled to the town of the Reb Elimelech. He yearned to hear any new stories he could find about him. Many years had already passed, and most people who knew the Reb Elimelech were already in the other world. However, there was one old person he found, a cook in the house of Reb Elimelech, who could remember one miraculous story. The servant said, "Each week before *shabbos*, the holy *rebbe* would enter the kitchen brokenhearted, filled with tears in his eyes. He would beg us all forgiveness saying, 'maybe I didn't show you enough respect or treat you right, forgive me forgive me... I promise I will do better. How can I enter *shabbos* without knowing all of you have forgiven me.'? Now you know he did nothing to us; he was the sweetest *rebbe,* but still, he felt he must aspire to improve and be there for us more. Not only this, when he left the room, we would all be trembling and crying; our knees would be knocking against each other until the candles of the holy *shabbos* were lit. With tears, we all begged each other forgiveness. As we probably didn't treat each other so well. It was *mamish* a scene just like on Eruv Yom Kippur. When the candles were lit, and *shabbos* finally arrived, our tears turned into immense joy. Each one of us felt it and we all tasted the joy of *shabbos;* experiencing a very great and elevated joy." (Or Zarua l'Tzaddik, quoted in Or ha-Shabbos, p. 48 n.)

So now my friends, do you forgive me? And I beg you to enter *shabbos* with forgiveness for your brothers and sisters.

Song of Songs

It is said of Rabbi Eleazar Zev of Kretchnif:

Before he went to say *Mincha* on *eruv shabbos*, he recited in his room, the Song of Songs slowly and with great *d'vekus*. (Raza d'Uvda, p. 24)

Flames of Fire

Our holy *rabbi* and master, Rabbi Tzvi of Ziditchov, blessed be his memory, once spent *shabbos* in Medzibuz. He wanted to see how the *rebbe* acted in his private room. So, he hid himself [in the *rebbe's*

73

room] along with another *chassid*, to hear the recital of the Song of Songs from the holy mouth of the *rebbe*, Reb Boruch. When Rabbi Boruch began the song, with fervor and longing, the other *chasssid* turned to Rabbi Tzvi, saying to him that his mind was becoming confused due to the great fire that was burning within him. When Rabbi Boruch recited the words, "His banner above me is love; support me with the trunks of the thickest trees, let me lean against the apple trees, for I am reeling with love," it appeared, as if fire was burning around the *rebbe*, and the *chassid* who was with Rabbi Tzvi fled because he could no-longer bear the great and awesome fire.

Rabbi Tzvi told us that he saw the sounds of the tongues of flame, and the house appeared altogether on fire. He reinforced himself and gathered his courage to hear the voice of that angel of *Hashem*. Upon arriving at the verse "I am my Beloved's and all His desire is for me" – then he almost went out of his mind. But our holy master, Rabbi Tzvi, thought to himself, "Whatever happens, I am ready to give my life to *Hashem*, with love, to hear these words of the Living *Hashem* as they were spoken at *Har Sinai*. If, G-d forbid, my soul leaves my body, I am prepared for whatever is the will of my Creator, blessed be He." Then there came upon him a new spirit from on high, and he saw the fire of *Hashem* flaming in the house in a way that cannot be described. He stood there until the *rebbe* said the words of the verse "For love is as strong as death, jealousy as cruel as hell; her coals are coals of fire; her flame is a mighty flame of *Hashem*." Then, because of the enormity of the fervor and longing, he almost passed out of existence, but *Hashem* was his aid until the whole of the Song of Songs was completed.

The holy *rabbi*, Rabbi Tzvi, always said that when it sometimes happens, G-d forbid, that he falls in his service of *Hashem*, from mental dimness or for other reasons, he recalls those precious moments when he heard the Song of Songs from the holy mouth of the Rebbe of Medzibuz. Then strength, and light, returns to his eyes because the words were like a flaming fire within his holy and pure heart. It was something unforgettable. (Yifrch biYamav Tzaddik, p. 55, #8)

What Does the *Rebbe* Teach You.

The Kotzker *chassid* asked his friend, "In what unique way does the Tchernobiler Rebbe teach his *chassdim*?" His comrade responded, "Our *rebbe* instructs us to stay awake all of Thursday night studying *Torah* until the sun rises. In the morning on, *erev shabbos*, we go to the *mikvah*, and then distribute *tzedakah*, everyone according to his ability and means. During the morning of *shabbos* we get together and

75

chant the entire Book of Psalms through, without an interruption." (Admorei Tchernobil, p. 150)

Pre-*Shabbos* Nap

Rabbi Mordechai of Lechovitz, may his merit protect us, was usually careful to take a nap *erev shabbos*. He did this as part of the honor of *shabbos*, in order to receive *shabbos*, with a clear mind and to be fully awake. (Or ha-Ner, p. 11, #1)

Shabbos in the Fields

One time, the Besht went with his holy disciples to welcome the *shabbos*. It was his way to always go out into the fields to do so. He did this in the early part of the afternoon, about two or three o'clock during summertime, and he would receive the *shabbos* there. (Adas Tzaddikim, p. 28)

The Feeling of True Revelation

I heard from my grandfather, of blessed memory, about the greatness of his *rebbe*, the holy master, Rabbi Yitzchok of Vorki, of blessed memory. He told me that when he heard him chanting *shalom aleichem* and *eshes chayil*, with the melodies he used, he could not at all imagine that the revelation on *Har Sinai* could have been more. For when the *Torah* was received at *Sinai*, when they heard from the mouth of the Holy One blessed be He, "I am the L-rd, thy G-d," and "Thou shalt not have any other gods before Me," etc. there was thundering and lightning. So, too was it when the Vorker Rebbe said and chanted *shalom alechem* and *eshes chayil*, for everyone there was a tremendous yearning for *Hashem*, and *d'vekus*, in fear and love of *Hashem*. (GMvGhTz, p. 30)

A Song Learned from the Angels

Once, on the night of *shabbos*, before the grace after meals, the holy Seer of Lublin was immersed in an awesome *d'vekus*. So much so, that he did so almost until expiration. After a few hours, he returned to normal consciousness and he began to sing the hymn "*l'El asher shavas* [To the G-d who rested]." He sang a completely new melody that the *chassidim* had never heard before. It was very beautiful, and everyone listened silently. The Seer told them afterwards that he had learned this *nigun* while he was deep in *d'vekus* [and in the Upper Worlds, having made a soul-ascent], from the angels who were singing before the Holy One, blessed be He. (Otzar Chayim, quoted in Or ha-Shabbos, p. 155)

77

Shabbos Dancing

It was the custom of the holy Rabbi Chayim of Kosov, every holy *shabbos* night, to lead dancing among those who stayed as guests at his pure table. This lasted for about an hour. (Even Shitiya, p. 48, #11)

Preparation to Eat

The *rabbi*, Reb [Yaakov] Koppel Hachassid, who in his youth lived in Kolomaya, made his living owning a small store. He was very hidden in his ways, such that no one knew of his great piety. Once, the Baal Shem Tov spent a *shabbos* in Kolomaya and during the evening of the holy *shabbos*, he felt a wondrous light flowing within the city. So, he went out to walk around the city to locate this great light of holiness. Eventually he found its location, near a small house. When he approached it, he felt the great light coming from within this house.

He entered, and he discovered there a beautiful pearl, namely Rabbi Koppel, who was singing and dancing. He was doing so for the glory and honor of the holy *shabbos*. With blazing devotion and without any weariness, he kept on dancing. He danced for one hour and then two, while the *shabbos* table was there laden with all sorts of delicacies. The Besht waited, not moving, beholding this sight for a long time.

When Rabbi Koppel finished his singing and dancing, he noticed the Baal Shem Tov standing there and he greeted him warmly. Full of joy he continued with the blessing of peace, and the Besht reciprocated the greeting with a similar warmth. Then the Besht inquired of him, "What is the meaning of this that you sing and dance so before you eat?" Rabbi Koppel responded to him, explaining how he does this at all three *shabbos* meals, at first simply standing before the table, singing and dancing. He does this so that first he delights in the spiritual aspect of the food, the holy vitality and life within it, and only afterwards does he eat. (Kol Sippurei Baal Shem Tov, vol. 4, p. 170)

Dancing Until *Shabbos* Morning

It is told of one of the descendants of Rabbi Naftali of Ropshitz, Rabbi Reuven Horowitz of Dembitz, that from the age of 12 he never slept on *shabbos*. Rather, throughout the night, he would dance before the *shabbos* queen. Not wanting him to go about the holiness himself, the townsfolk organized themselves into four groups, to sing and dance with him during each of the four watches of the night. (Ohel Naftali, p. 31, #75)

The Entire Book of Psalms

It was the custom of the *rebbetzin*, the *tzaddekes* Feigele [whose husband was Rabbi Dovid Moshe of Tchorkov] to recite the entire Book of Psalms the night of *shabbos*. (Tiferes Adam, p. 11)

To Sleep or Not to Sleep

Of the *rebbe*, Rabbi Meir Shalom of Kolishin (the grandson of the Holy Jew of Pshischa):

His way was to remain awake the entire night of *shabbos and* occupy himself with *Torah* and the service of *Hashem*. (Tiferes Banim Avotam, p. 223)

The Tzanzer Rebbe would often say: "It is a pity to sleep on the night of the holy *shabbos* — for you lose the special illumination of *shabbos*. It is also a great *tikkun* for the soul on the night of *shabbos* when you sing songs and praises to *Hashem*, blessed be He." He went on to explain the practice of sleeping the minimum on *shabbos* with a parable of a wise king who slept little, saying, "It is a pity to lose his kingship — for when he is asleep, he is not a king." But for all that, the Tzanzer did sleep some on the night of *shabbos*, so that he could pray with a clear head in the morning. (Rabbeinu ha-Kodesh mi-Tzanz, p.221)

Repeating 'Holy *Shabbos*'

About Rabbi Eleazar Zev of Kretchnif:

On *shabbos* he would remark many times, softly but with great devotion, "Holy *shabbos*, Holy *shabbos*," over and over. (Raza d'Uvda, p. 28)

The *admor*, Rebbe of Parisov, of blessed memory, would go around the entire night of the holy *shabbos*, saying again and again without cease, "Holy *shabbos*, His precious day," [*Shabbos Kodesh, yom hemdaso*]. (Vayakel Shlomo, *p. 16*)

The Words of *Shabbos*

Rabbi Mordechai of Neshkiz was very careful about not speaking any profane words on *shabbos* and would strongly caution others about this as well. (Zichron l'Rishonim, p. 105)

Holy *Shabbos* Talk

About the Maggid of Mezritch:

His custom was, on *shabbos* and holidays, to speak [only] in *lashon hakodesh*. (Imrei Pinchas, p. 14)

81

Trembling *Kiddush* Hands

On the evening of the holy *shabbos*, during the *kiddush*, I saw with my own eyes how our glorious master, teacher and Rabbi Shlomo Leib of Lentsho, may his merit protect us, said the Name in the blessing over the wine. While doing so, a great fear of *Hashem* came upon him. So much so, that all his limbs trembled, and the cup of wine dropped from his hand. It did not fall to the ground, however, because he managed to restrain it with his other hand. But, needless to say, the wine spilled, and he was forced to refill the cup. Then, he finished saying the *kiddush* in a loud voice, as was his holy way. From that day forward, the *rebbe* never held the cup by himself, but rather rested his hands on the back of the chair with the cup on them, and someone else would hold the cup steady on his hands. And though we know that the *tzaddikim* have such fear and awe of *Hashem* always, without a moment's cessation, yet they keep it hidden within themselves so that it not be seen – but this time the *rebbe* could not hold it inside. (Emunas Tzaddikim, p. 87)

Fear of Heaven

It is told of the holy Rabbi Yaakov Koppel Chassid of Kolomaya, a disciple of the Besht and founder of the *chassidic* dynasty of Kosov -Vishnitz, that he would verbally repeat at all hours of the day, nonstop, "I have placed the L-rd before me always." He even did this during the hours of work and business. So much so that even the gentiles called him "The *Shivittinik*," recognizing his fear of Heaven. (Tiferes Beis Dovid, p.103)

A *Yichud* with Coins

As a young child, Rebbe Nachman of Breslov, would often take several silver coins and have them exchanged for copper ones. Afterwards, he would secretly enter the synagogue through the window, taking along his copy of [the prayer book] *Shaarey Tzion*. Then he would joyfully recite the prayer, *Leshem Yichud* ["For the sake of the unification of the Holy One, blessed be He, and His *Shechinah*, etc.."], petitioning that the elements of *Hashem's* Name be united through the good deed he was about to perform. As soon as he completed the prayer, he would grab one copper coin and place it in the charity box for anonymous donors. Immediately afterwards, he would distract himself, as if he had completed the deed and was ready to leave. Then suddenly, he would begin all over again. He would say the *Leshem Yichud* a second time and deposit yet another coin in the alms box. Repeatedly, he would distract himself until he had placed every single piece of copper in the donation box, each time repeating the *Leshem Yichud*. In this very simple and unsophisticated manner, he

83

would perform not one, but many *mitzvos* using just a single silver coin. (Rabbi Nachman's Wisdom, p. 13, Shevachey HaRan, #13)

Blessing with *Kavana*

It is said of Rabbi Levi Yitzchak of Berditchev:

His way in holiness resembled that of a fiery angel. It was told of him that when some food was brought before him to eat, he had to make a blessing of enjoyment first. So, he began by making the blessing with such fervor, and with such a great fire of devotion, that he would end up in one corner of the room and the food in the other corner. (Seder ha-Doros ha-Chadash, p.36)

Always for the Poor

We are told in the *midrash* about Rabbi Tanchum:

If he was going to buy one liter of meat, he would purchase two liters instead; one portion for himself and one portion for the poor.

Learning How to Speak in Holiness

Our holy master, the Holy Jew of Pshischa, sent a message with some *chassidim*, that they should come to him. So, they traveled to Pshischa, and upon arriving near the city at dusk, they came across their *rebbe*, the Holy Jew. The *rebbe* had gone out for a walk in the countryside with some disciples. When the *chassidim* noticed their master, they jumped out of the carriage, and ran to him to receive the greeting of peace. However, when the Holy Jew greeted them, he remarked, "Young men, why don't I see any of your words?" [With his spiritual insight, he did not see that these *chassidim* had any hold in the World of Speech.] The *chassidim* answered simply, "Why should we speak unnecessarily? Isn't it better instead just to speak words in learning *Torah* and praying?" Seeing a greater potential for them, his holy master responded, "If that's the situation, prepare a pipe for yourselves, and get enough tobacco for the whole night; come to me after the evening prayers, and I'll teach you how to speak." As spoken, the *rebbe* and *chassidim* sat together the entire night, while the *rebbe* taught them how to speak. After this, they began to talk again. (Ohel Elimelech, p. 72, #172)

Binding Their Words

Rabbi Israel Baal Shem Tov remarked, "Sometimes when I am sitting among people who are conversing idly, I first attach myself in *d'vekus* with *Hashem*, blessed be He. Then, I bind all their words

with greater attachment [to their spiritual roots.]"
(Likkuti Yekarim, p. 5a)

You Just Don't Want to

Once, when the Holy Jew of Pshischa was
taking a stroll through the countryside with his
disciples, they came across a hay wagon that had
overturned. The gentile driver called out to them to
assist him in putting it upright and reloading the hay.
They went to help him, but try as they could, they
were unable to turn it over. "We can't do it," the
chassidim told him. Not believing them, the gentile
yelled at them angrily in Polish, "You can all right, but
you don't want to!" When he was done, then the Holy
Jew turned to his disciples and said, "Do you hear
what this gentile is saying? He says, we can lift up the
Shechinah from the dust, but we don't want to." (Sichos
Chayim, p. 9)

A Glow From Speaking Little

There is nothing as beneficial for purifying the
soul as keeping a reign over your mouth and
eschewing idle conversation. Not only for purity
reasons, but it benefits you greatly in having *kavanah*
in prayer, as alien thoughts become unable to intrude
and distract you.

There is a story of a *chassid* who, following his death, showed himself to his wife in a dream. Upon seeing the hair of his head and beard all aglow like a torch, in his glory, she was taken aback, knowing full well that he was an average person. She asked him, "By what did you merit all this?" He explained, "It was because I spoke as little as possible of things other than *Torah* and the fear of *Hashem* – for the Holy One, blessed be He, is sure to care for those who exert themselves to avoid profane talk." (Kav ha-Yashar, chap. 12)

A Reminder to Watch One's Tongue

Rabbi Yosi Ber, of Brisk, would always keep a snuffbox on this table. Whenever he was about to converse with someone, he would first open it up, glance within, and only then begin to speak. One of his close disciples could no longer overcome his curiosity and took a glance inside. There he found engraved the abbreviation W.K.H.M.A.T.K.H.F.T. Not knowing what this meant, he bravely questioned the *rabbi* about it. He answered, "It is from the verse of scripture, 'Who so keeps his mouth and tongue, keeps himself from trouble.'" [Proverbs 21:23. (Midor Dor, vol. 2, #1619)

Refusing to Hear Idle Conversation

About Rabbi Shlomo Leib of Lentshno:

He never engaged in any idle conversation; even from his youth he was careful about this. He would guard himself against hearing idle talk, and even more so, profane speech, *chas v'shalom.*

While he was young he was living with a tailor, and he would not return to the house until all were asleep. One time, during the bitter frigid winter, it happened that they closed the *beis medrash* early for some reason, and [not being able to stay there to study and pray] he was forced to return home.

Upon approaching the shared house, however, he heard the tailor, as usual, still at work with his young helpers. Also, as usual, which is why he normally stayed late in the *beis medrash*, they were talking about indecent and unclean things. As a result, Rabbi Shlomo refused to enter. Instead, he stayed outside walking this way and that, for it was very cold outside. He became so cold that he almost died. He found himself just laying down on the earth from weakness. However, despite this, he would still not go in, for he was determined that he would not hear idle conversation. While he lay there almost lifeless, a miracle occurred, and the one candle they had inside went out. Having no choice, the workers were forced to finish for the night and retire early to sleep. Seeing this, he finally went inside. "From then on," the holy Rabbi Shlomo said, "my ears developed the ability to hear what people are whispering even at far distances." (Eser Atarot, p. 21, #3)

A Melody as Part of Every Discourse

Rabbi Shneur Zalman of Liadi noticed an elderly gentleman among his listeners. It was clear from the man's expression that he did not comprehend the meaning of his discourse. So, he summoned him to his side and told him, "I see that my sermon is unclear to you. Listen to this melody, and it will teach you how to cleave to the L-rd." Reb Shneur Zalman then began to sing a song without using words. It was a song of *Torah*, of trust in *Hashem*, of longing for the L-rd, and of love for Him.

"I understand now what you wish to teach," explained the old man. "I feel an intense longing to be united with the L-rd."

The *rebbe*'s melody became part of his every discourse henceforth, although it had no words. (BeOhalei Chabad, pp. 49-50)

Dancing at Every Occasion

The Holy Grandfather [of Shpola] was known for dancing on *shabbos* and holidays. However, it wasn't just then. Every occasion of a *mitzvah*, and of inspiration, became a time of ecstatic dancing, even while the fish were frying, when he himself cooked them in honor of the holy *shabbos*. (Ish ha-Pele, p. 75)

Dancing Through the Night

It is told of Rabbi Chayim of Tzanz:

Once during *shabbos* evening, he poured himself the wine for *kiddush*, took the cup in his hand, and began to sing. He did so with tremendous fervor and holy awe. He would sing the words, "O Creator, You are the Crown; O Creator, You are the Crown," for more than an hour. He continued in this way, until the thick candles that were burning on the table went out – but he, with great *d'vekus*, kept on singing. (Rabbeinu ha-Kodesh mi-Tzanz, p. 219)

Dancing Like an Angel

About Rabbi Moshe Leib of Sassov it is said:

The spectacle of his dancing on the night of *shabbos* was like a wondrous vision. It was something not of this world. Every *shabbos* evening, he took expensive new shoes, put them on, and began dancing for the honor of the holy *shabbos* queen. His dancing was not a regular type, but rather a dancing of *d'vekus*, of yearning and thirsting for *Hashem* until expiration. With every movement he would make, he accomplished awesome and wondrous unifications, until the whole house was full of light. All the heavenly host of angels danced along with him, a great fire flamed around him, and it was seen that the *Shechinah* came to rest in his *beis medrash*.

He would be robed all in white, and his face appeared like that of an angel of *Hashem*. For hours at a time he danced in simplicity, utterly divorced from all materiality, without tiring. His dancing drew the attention of all the *chassidim* of Apta, where he was living. Never did they tire of watching the revelation of the *Shechinah* that took place where he danced. (Tiferes Banim Avotam, p. 177)

Making the Right Choice With Tears

Rabbi Yitzchok Isaac of Komarna wrote about his early adolescence:

"I went through a brief period, where I experienced a great strengthening of *Samael* [Satan], may his name be blotted out, and I failed to guard my eyes. There loomed before me two paths, one to

Gehinnom and one to *Gan Eden,* and I had to choose. Then the side of good was aroused inside me, and one day I entered the *shul* alone, and cried my heart out before Him who created the world. The tears flowed from my eyes as if falling from a fountain, until I fainted. I can tell you, from that day until today, twenty-fire years later, I have not looked at, or seen even at a glance, the visage of a married women. Since then, I have heavenly aid that I will not see this even by chance. After that experience, I returned to my service of *Hashem,* to *Torah* and to prayer." (Ateret Tiferet, p. 32, #23)

Earth, Earth, You are Better Than I

This is what Rabbi Zusha of Hanipol did. In order to humble himself, he would say, "Earth, Earth, you are better than I, and yet how is it that I walk on you and trample you with my feet? Soon the time will come when I will lie under you and be subject to you." (Derech Emunah u'Maaseh Rav, p. 20)

Be the Master

About Rabbi Mendel of Premishlan, it is said that the way he achieved his spiritual perfection was by means of interruptions. He would interrupt his vision [by turning away or closing his eyes while looking at something], and so on in many other things. He did so in order to reach self-mastery of his eyes, and other senses. (Derech Tzaddikim, p. 4, #21)

Stopping Up His Ears

Aaron, the son of Rabbi Chayim of Amdur, was nicknamed the deaf Reb Arele because he had stopped up his ears for such a long time. Just as the Seer of Lublin covered his eyes for a long time until eventually his physical vision became poor, as is famous, so the holy Reb Arele stopped up his ears, and as a result, he talked very little. (Shema Shlomo, II, p. 30, #58)

Removing the Mask

When Rabbi Yaakov Yitzchok of Lublin [the Seer] was 12 years old, he accepted upon himself not to look outside of his personal space [four *amos*]. To accomplish this, he tied a handkerchief over his eyes. This was so that he could not see more than what was below or around his legs. He went about that way for two and a half years, until Rabbi Shmelke, his *rebbe*, instructed him to stop. He explained to him, that avoiding the light of evil is not the true service of the *tzaddik*. The essence of Divine service is when you control yourself from doing evil and overcome it. "And," continued Rabbi Shmelke, "a *tzaddik* needs to refine his limbs and train them so that even with his eyes fully open he will not notice evil, and with his ears he will hear no evil talk." (Ha-Hozeh mi-Lublin, p. 20)

Rabbi Shmelke said of him that in those two years he attained all his spiritual levels. Because it was there he taught himself that his vision and his speech should be dedicated to the service of *Hashem* alone. As we know from future stories of him, his spiritual vision was profound. (Niflaos ha-Rebbe, p. 50, #102, #104; p. 51, #106; p. 71, #185)

Only See What Has Purpose

The Lubliner taught his eyes not to see whatsoever that had no purpose for his service of *Hashem*. In *Derech Pikudecha* it is written [by Rabbi Tzvi Elimelech of Dinov]: "I witnessed with my own eyes how our holy master and *rebbe*, Rabbi Yaakov Yitzchok of Lublin, of blessed memory, had his eyes completely within his control. He could look directly at something, if it had no relation to his service of *Hashem*, he wouldn't notice it. In truth, what I saw of this cannot even be described in mere words." (Niflaos ha-Rebbe, p. 92, #315; p. 94, #324)

Don't Consider Yourself Wise nor Clever With the Eyes

Simcha Bunim of Kalish [in the Vorki line of *chassidic rebbes*] was once walking with the *tzaddik*, Rabbi Dovid Biderman of Lelov, in the paths of Jerusalem. It was his holy way that his eyes were covered with a large cloth [when he went about outside], and Rabbi Dovid had to lead him to their destination.

When they arrived, Rabbi Dovid questioned why he did this. "Was it not possible to keep your eyes from looking on bad things, without covering them?"

"What!" responded Rabbi Simcha Bunim, shaking all over. "Is it not written, 'Be not wise in [with] your own eyes?' When it comes to the holiness of the eyes, you are not to consider yourself wise and clever.'" (Ha-Tzaddik ha-Shotek, p. 110)

Mentioning with Respect

It is told about the Maggid of Koznitz:

When he was learning *gemara* with his *talmidim*, he would mention the name of a *Tanna* or an *Amora* or even just a *posek* [a halachic authority], he would mention them with awe and reverence. He made sure to call them, the holy Rava, the holy Rashi, the holy *Tosafos*, and other similar language. (Eser Oros, p. 69, #9)

Say *Be'ezras* Hashem

A certain rich man had a lot of land, but he had no oxen with which to plough it. So, what did he do? He took his wallet full of money and went to another city to the market to purchase some oxen.

It is accurate to say that this man was very generous, giving a lot of charity, and always offering hospitality in his home. However, his heart was not firm in believing in *Hashem's* Divine Providence over all things. After being generous to others, he would often think to himself in a proud way that, "It is my own doing and ability which have brought me all this wealth," for he had made an abundant amount of money.

On his way to the other town, he was met by Elijah the prophet, who was disguised as a peddler going to market. Elijah asked the man, "Where are you going?" He responded that he was going to the market to purchase some oxen. The old man said to him, "Say, '*Be'ezras Hashem*, G-d willing' or 'If G-d, blessed be He, so decrees.'" However, the man gave no heed to the advice, responding "My money is in

my wallet and it all depends on my will." Elijah
responded, "If that is your attitude, then you are not
going to be successful in this."

Not so long after, the rich man's wallet fell out
of his pocket without his noticing it. Elijah then
picked it up and placed it under a large rock deep in
the forest, in a place where no one ever passed.

When the man made a deal for some oxen at
the market, and reached for his wallet to pay, he
realized that he had misplaced it while traveling and
went home in disappointment. Again, he took more
money from his safe and went to the market to buy
oxen. Once again Elijah the prophet, who was also
going to the market, met him. However, this time
appearing like a different old man.

Elijah asked him, "Where are you going sir?"
The merchant answered that he was going to the
market to purchase some oxen. The old man
answered back, "Say, *'Be'ezras Hashem*, G-d willing' or
'If *Hashem*, blessed be He, so decrees.'" However, the
man continued his stubbornness, giving the same
answer as he did the first time.

Elijah, who was sent from *Hashem* to fix this
man's perspective, caused sleepiness to descend upon
him. The merchant sat down to rest and quickly fell

into a deep slumber. Then, once asleep, without the merchant feeling anything, Elijah removed his wallet with the money out of his pocket. He then left it in the middle of the forest for safekeeping, along with the previous funds.

When the merchant awoke, and noticed that his money had disappeared yet again, he said to himself, "It must have been that robbers came along and stole my wallet." Once again, he went home in disappointment.

While repeating his way through the trail home, it finally dawned upon him: "No, this must be *Hashem's* hand causing this to happen because I haven't believed with complete faith in the Divine Providence of the Creator, blessed be He." So, he decided then and there that from that day forward, he would always say "*Be'ezras Hashem*" for everything he planned to do.

So, the merchant tried a third time with his new dedication to *Hashem,* taking a wallet full of money to go to the market to buy oxen. Again, Elijah met him on the road, this time in the guise of a poor youth who was looking to hire himself out for some work. The boy asked the merchant, "Where is my master going?" He responded happily, "I'm going to the market to buy oxen, *Be'ezras Hashem.*" Elijah, who was the boy, blessed him with success in his purchase and requested of him, "Let me ask you just one thing, master. When you purchase the oxen and require a helper to drive them to your home, perhaps you'll be kind enough to hire me for the work? I'll be at the market too, and I'm very poor and it's that kind of work that I'm setting my hopes on." The merchant said to him gladly, "Fine, if *Be'ezras Hashem*, I buy some oxen, come to me then and I'll take you on to help me drive them home."

The merchant did indeed purchase good oxen, and cheaply too. As promised, he hired Elijah, the boy, to lead the oxen home. While traveling on the road, they were passing alongside the large forest with the oxen, and in the middle of the journey the oxen stampeded, fleeing into the depths of the forest. The merchant and the boy chased after them but, unable to catch up to them, the oxen went farther and farther into the woods. They stopped however, when they came to the crag of the large rock on which the two earlier wallets, with the money, were placed.

Finally, when the merchant caught up with the animals, he noticed his wallets with the money still in them and was overcome with joy. He immediately gave full praise to *Hashem*, right there and then. Following this, his oxen went along calmly, listening to the commands of those leading them, until finally the merchant returned safely to his home. Then, suddenly, the boy vanished into thin air. The heart of the merchant was opened, and he understood that it was nothing but Providence from Above that was behind all this. About himself, he said the verse, "It is an ignorant man who will not know, and a fool who will not understand this." (Psalms 92:7) (Otzar ha-Sippurim, V, story 8)

Interrupting His *D'vekus*

Once, when the holy *gaon* Rabbi Avraham Dovid of Butchatch, went to the bathroom [outhouse], one of his opponents locked the door on him from the outside so that he was stuck there for an hour. The holy *tzaddik*, of blessed memory, suffered very much from the unpleasant odor, also from the fact that he had to constrain his mind from thinking holy thoughts all that time; for he never ceased for a moment from thinking holy thoughts in *d'vekus* with the Creator of all worlds.

When the people of the *rebbe's* household realized that he was missing, they found him and opened the door for him. They told him that for the sake of the honor of Heaven, and the honor of the *Torah*, he should take revenge on his opponents and put them under a ban. He was about to follow their advice and took a *shofar* in his hand to blow in invoking the ban. Then something turned within him, 'perhaps you are concerned with this holy man?' He put down the *shofar* and decided to simply move on. (Sefer ha-Dorot ha-Chadash, p. 10)

Finding a *Mitzvah*

We find in the *Talmud Eruvin* [28b], that when Rabbi Zera would feel tired and weak, and could not study *Torah* or do any other *mitzvah*, he would go and sit at the entrance of the house of Rabbi Yuda, the son of Rabbi Ammi. There he would say, "When the *rabbis* come to his house and leave, I'll be able to stand before them [to give them honor] as they go in and out — so I won't be idle without doing any *mitzvos.*" [It is a *mitzvah* to stand up this way to honor *Torah* scholars.]

I have received a tradition from holy people, that if they were for some time unable to do any other *mitzvah*, they would handle their *tzitzis* and look at them. Why? Because looking at the *tzitzis* is something very deep and lifts up the *Shechinah* which is in exile. (Kav ha-Yashar, chap. 45, beginning)

Sleep, the Backup Plan

The holy Rabbi Mordechai, of Nadvorna, once remarked, "I have to give myself credit that when I was young, as long as I had strength in my legs to carry my body, I never lay down to sleep." He only slept

101

when he absolutely was falling off his feet and had no strength at all – and he would sleep once every two days. (Raza d'Uvda, Sh'ar ha-Osiyos, *p. 77, #2*)

Waking Up Reb Elimelech

Since it was improper for the *chassidim* to awaken their *rebbe*, they asked Rabbi Zusha, his older brother, to perform the task. So, Rabbi Zusha accompanied them to the room where Rabbi Elimelech was sleeping. He stood at the doorway and put his hand over the *mezuzah*. To the astonishment of all, Rabbi Elimelech instantly woke up. They asked Rabbi Zusha to explain the reason for this, and he said the following:

"It is well known that you are supposed to picture the name *YKVK* continuously before your eyes, as it says, 'I have placed the Lord [*YKVK*] before me always.' How then could a man go to sleep, for during sleep it is impossible to do this?" Answering his own question, he said, "The answer is that we rely on the Divine Name which is written on the *mezuzah* [the letter *shin* on the outside which stands for *shakai*, the Almighty]. So, when I placed my hand on the *mezuzah* and covered up the Name, Rabbi Elimelech had to awaken immediately in order to picture *YKVK* before his eyes." (Ohel Elimelech, p. 49, #124)

An Allotted Time for Sleeping

Once, when the holy Rabbi Mordechai, of Nadvorna, wanted to teach his *chassidim* a way in the service of *Hashem*. He told them that before he went to sleep he decided beforehand exactly how much time he wanted to sleep. Should he then have overslept even a little beyond what he had decided, he penalized himself by decreasing his sleep the next day. (Raza d'Uvda, Sh'ar ha-Osiyos, p. 77, #3)

Nightly Accounting

During daytime, Reb Zusha, may his merit protect us, wrote everything he did on a slip of paper. Before retiring to sleep at night, he read it over and wept until the writing was blurred by his tears. At that point, he knew that his sins were forgiven. From this story, we can see how everyone should be a Master of Accounts every night before sleep. (Knesset Yisrael, p. 136)

A Fine-Tooth Comb

It is told of Rabbi Levi Yitzchok of Berditchev:

Before going to bed each night, he searched his actions of the day and went over them carefully. He considered them so closely, with such a fine-tooth comb, that he always found faults in everything he did. To do *teshuva* for this, he would say aloud, "But Levi Yitzchok - didn't you say the same thing last night?" Then he would answer himself, "Yes, but yesterday I wasn't telling the truth and now I am!" (Zichron l'Rishonim, p.96)

Be Careful of Your Deeds

The holy Rabbi Yitzchok was on the level that, immediately upon laying down in bed, he said the words "Into Your hands I commend my spirit," and he would immediately fall asleep. Should it happen that he did not immediately fall asleep, he would know that he had committed some sin, and they did not want to receive him in heaven until he had done *teshuva*. For during sleep the soul of a righteous person ascends Above.

Once this happened, and he considered his deeds of the day, finding no fault of his own. So, he continued, and scrutinized his deeds even more carefully. Finally, he realized that he had been together with some people [*misnagdim*] who made fun of the Baal Shem Tov, and he had kept quiet, not protesting their unfavorable words.

Without further thought, he promptly arose from his bed and gave orders to his coachman to prepare the coach. Immediately, they set out during the night for the holy community of Medzibuz, to ask the Besht for forgiveness. Now, the Besht had never met Rabbi Yitzchok, and no one at all in Medzibuz knew about him. Rabbi Yitzchok arrived in the very early hours of the morning and went directly to the *beis medrash* to pray. He was standing in the far corner of the *beis medrash* out of notice, praying quietly, thinking he would approach the *rav* after *davening*. However, when they took out the *sefer Torah* to read, the Besht called him up for an *aliyah* by name, addressing him as "Our master and teacher, Rabbi Yitzchok, the son of Rabbi Yosef." Then turning to him, the Baal Shem Tov said to him in a sweet voice, along with a gentle humor and a smile on his lips, "Is it worth making fun of the Besht if you have to travel such a distance to make amends? Don't worry though, the Besht forgives you completely, from his heart."

Look carefully at this story of how great was the holiness of Rabbi Yitzchok, and how careful he was about the least suggestion of slander. [Think twice next time you hear something or speak words of slander.] (Mazkeret Shem ha-Gedolim, p. 4)

I Forgive You, *Rebbe*

A wondrous story was told by Rabbi Zusha of Hanipoli, who had been a disciple of Rabbi Yechiel

Michel of Zlotchov, the son of Rabbi Yitzchok of Drobitch.

When I was young, and a disciple of Rabbi Yechiel Michal of Zlotchov, my holy *rebbe* once spoke to me harshly. Afterwards, however, he completely apologized and asked, "Reb Zusha, forgive me for humiliating you." I answered him, "*Rebbe*, of course I forgive you!"

However, before I went to sleep that night, he came to me again, and again said, "Reb Zusha, forgive me!" And once again I answered him, "I forgive you, *rebbe*!"

Finally, I went to bed that night as usual, however something happened. When I closed my eyes, the *rebbe*'s father, the holy Rabbi Yitzchok of Drobitch, of blessed memory, came to me from the Upper World [he was deceased] and appeared to me while I was still awake. He said to me in a concerned tone, "I have only one son in the Lower World, a precious and wonderful son, and you want to destroy him because he insulted you!" I answered him, "*Rebbe*! Haven't I already forgiven him with all my heart and soul? What more can I do?" He responded, "That is still not a complete forgiveness. Come with me and I'll show you how to forgive!"

I got up and followed him until we arrived at
the *mikvah*. There Reb Yitzchok told me to immerse
three times, and each time to say that I forgave his
son. I did so, and when I got out of the *mikvah* I saw
that his face was shining with such a great light that I
wasn't able to look at him. (Tosafot ha-Rim, p. 174)

Repeating *Shema*

Rabbi Shmuel [bar Nahmeni would] recite the
shema in bed, and then repeat it over and over until he
fell asleep while in the middle of saying it. (Yerushalmi
Brachos, 1-13)

Calling Out, Holy Father

After relating to his *chassidim* how Rabbi Dovid
Moshe of Tchortkov slept only two hours at night, a
chassidic story goes on to say:

Even during that time, he would continually
call out while sleeping, "Holy Father! Holy Master of
the entire world," just as was his holy practice during
meals, when he sat at his pure table before *Hashem*, in
the company of his *chassidim*. (Eser Oros, p. 147, 8)

Talking in His Sleep

A disciple of Rabbi Mordechai of Lechovitz:
107

Reb Moshe Steinerman

Our master, the holy grandfather Rabbi Mordechai, testified about Rabbi Moshe Binyamin. He said that five minutes would never pass by without him thinking about *teshuva* and turning to *Hashem*.

One time, Rabbi Mordechai sent his great disciple Rabbi Moshe of Kobrin to Rabbi Moshe Binyamin, so that he could learn from him directly how a Jew should sleep. The Kobriner was with him in his bedroom and saw how while sleeping he would wake up every few minutes and cry out from his great *d'vekus*, "Master of the World!" and other things like that. (Toras Avos, Maasei Avos – Ha-Saba Kadisha mi-Lechovitz, 23)

Small Interruptions of Sleep

It is told of Rabbi Dovberish, the *maggid* of Lublin:

His holy way was to study *Torah* with his son from memory. Every *shabbos*, they would study together until the candles went out. When he went to sleep, he would tell his son Eliezar also to go to sleep. Side by side, with a little partition between the two beds, they slept. There was water next to each bed so that they could wash upon awakening. Together, they would learn *Torah* in the dark until they began to doze off a little, just like [in the Talmud Brachos 3b] King David did, making sure 30 minutes didn't pass without awakening. Suddenly, a few minutes later after resting, the *maggid* would wash his hands and call out to his son in a loud voice, "*Lazerka, Lazerka,* you have already slept too much. Now is the time to learn!"

Again, they began learning *Torah* together until they dozed off. Once again, he would awaken, wake his son and learn with him. This happened every night, and so did they pass the entire night in learning, with small interruptions of sleep. (Shemen ha-Tov, p. 100)

A Master's Sleep

About Rabbi Yitzchok Issac of Ziditchov, we are told:

Our master's day commenced half an hour, or an hour before midnight (on days that he did not stay awake all night) and ended at 9 P.M. During his youth he would not go to sleep at all but would just doze off briefly while sitting in his chair with a book of *Torah* in his hand. Later, he strengthened himself like a lion, putting his feet in a basin of cold water in order to keep himself awake. He stood that way throughout the night studying *Torah*, his feet remaining in the bucket.

These acts of piety continued even in his old age, when he was weak and was forced to sleep in a bed, even then he would only sleep in short spurts until midnight. After sleeping about fifteen minutes, he would wake and wash his hands three times, then return to sleep for another sixty breaths [the *rabbis* said that a horse only dozes off for sixty breaths at a time] as at first. Then he would wake up again and wash again. This was his holy way of sleep until midnight. As soon as midnight struck he awoke fully, got up from his bed, and began his Divine service. (Pe'er Yitzchok, p.78, #1)

Sleeping with a *Sefer*

About Rabbi Menachem Mendel of Rimanov it is told:

He never passed midnight in sleep, and the time that he slept until midnight was in this manner. Beside him he had the books he was studying placed on the table near his bed. When he had slept five or ten minutes, he awoke and washed his hands (his personal attendant who sat near his bed handed him the vessel of water). Then he would study for five or six minutes in a somewhat hurried way in the book he had ready. Afterwards, he lay down and fell asleep instantly. After sleeping for some more minutes, he awoke, washed his hands, and studied another book – the *Zohar*, or *Mishna*, etc. Thus, did he do for the length of those hours he slept, until midnight. (Ateres Menachem, p. 35, #116)

But as For Me, I Can't Sleep.

The Tzanzer Rebbe also slept very little. When he got up from his meager nap, he did so with such vigor that he almost leapt out of bed. A few times he got into bed, having taken off all his clothes, even his socks, and then, after having slept only two or three minutes, he got up!

One time, a great *rabbi* expressed his frustration to him, saying that, try as he might, he was unable to overcome his need and desire for sleep. He questioned the Tzanzer, if there was a method that he used, that enabled him to function with so little sleep. Since this *rabbi* heard about the Tzanzer's ways with sleep, it was understandable that he asked him what he could do to be like him.

Our holy *rabbi* answered him, saying "If you are able to sleep, how good. But as for me, I can't sleep. (Mekor Chayim, p. 101) Meaning that it wasn't that he was trying not to sleep, as much as his *avodas Hashem* in *Torah* study meant so much to him, that he was unable to simply allow the time to pass.

The *Mikvah* of *D'vekus*

Once, the holy Yismach Moshe [Rabbi Moshe Teitelbaum] was with the holy Seer of Lublin in a town without a normal *mikvah*. So, the Yismach Moshe decided to use the nearby river. Afterwards, he went to where his *rebbe* was staying, to greet him. The Seer noticed that water was still dripping from his beard and *payos*. He asked him how he went to the *mikvah*; was it not in ruins?

When Rabbi Moshe explained that he had gone to the river to immerse, the Seer said, "And what is one to do if there is no *mikvah*, or also no river? Then you can immerse yourself in the River of Fire." And he whispered into the ear of his disciple, "in the fire of *d'vekus*." (Eser Oros, p. 98, #66)

The *Mikvah* River of Fire

The holy Rabbi Moshe of Kobrin was once praising the *tzaddik* [Rabbi Yisrael] of Ruzhin in the highest way. He told a story how he was once sitting next to him on *shabbos*, close to nightfall. Suddenly out of nowhere, the *rebbe* said to him, "A Jew must learn how to immerse in the River of Fire!"

"And immediately," said the holy Rabbi Moshe, "the Rizhiner Tzaddik bent over [as if immersing] three times, and when he straightened up, water was dripping from his *payos!*" (Beis Rizhin, p. 206)

The Waters of Wisdom

The Kotzker Rebbe had no opportunity to go to the *mikvah* before *shabbos*, nor could he do so in the evening, and he was very upset about this. Then he decided what to do; he would use the *kabbalistic* intentions for the *mikvah*, meditating on them in depth, as if he were actually immersing in the *mikvah*. "Because," he said to himself, "the essence of the immersion is the spiritual purity attained through purification in the waters of wisdom. Therefore, there is no absolute necessity for the actual material waters, and the movement of the bodily limbs in the water. The spiritual immersion can be accompanied by the removal of all materiality, and the body, from the soul as a garment [*hispashtus ha-gashmiyus*], and together with it the fullest concentration of the mind in the intentions of the Upper Immersion."

As he began his meditation, he concentrated all his powers to meditate on all the exalted intentions and thoughts connected with the *mikvah*, with the holy names of *Hashem* related to it. He stripped himself of all external thoughts, pacing back and forth in the *beis medrash* until he felt within himself that he had completed his task, and that a new spirit had been

113

born within him and he had become another man. (Shivhei Tzaddikim, p. 43)

A Night Time Ritual

The holy Rabbi Chaim of Tzanz would go to the *mikvah* before reciting the midnight service. When he returned from the *mikvah*, he began saying *tikkun chatzos* with an outpouring of his soul, and with such bitter crying that those who were outside his room would themselves break down and begin to wail. Following the *tikkun*, he learned the *Zohar* with great *d'vekus*, and then he repeated *mishniyos* from memory, usually from the order of *zeraim*. (Sefer Rabbeinu ha-Kodesh mi-Tzanz, p. 250)

What Kind of Fire is it?

When the Baal Shem Tov was first married, he made his living by the labor of his hands and was very poor. Once during his travels, for several days he was on the farm of a charitable Jew, who had a special cottage for poor people who needed hospitality and assistance.

Following the holy *shabbos*, when Reb Baruch [the landowner] lay down to go to sleep, he suddenly and unexpectedly noticed a light through his window. He picked himself up out of bed and went over to the window to see where it was coming from. When he saw that there was a bright light coming from one of the rooms of the poor people's house, he became worried. Reb Baruch was very afraid, for he thought maybe, G-d forbid, a fire had broken out. So, he grabbed his clothes and quickly dressed. He ran outside to locate the problem and to see where this light came from. As he approached the door of the room, he did so carefully so as not to awaken anyone else. Looking through the keyhole, he saw the poor man [the Baal Shem Tov] sitting on the ground and reciting, with great trembling, the *Tikkun Chatzos* midnight prayer. He was holding by the verse, "Why have you forgotten us for so long? Why have You left us for so long, and why have You left us abandoned for such length of days?" His hands were spread and raised, his face was shining brightly with a great light, and tears were running down his cheeks. (Sippurei Chassidim, Zevin, vol. I, #268) So there was no actual fire like Reb Boruch thought; however, he now understood that his guest was a holy *tzaddik*.

Taking Care of the Widows

It was the custom of Reb Moshe Leib of Sassov, each day after the morning prayers, to go to all the widows of the city and to wish them a good morning. (Menorah ha-Tehorah, p. 51, #7)

Once, there was a very poor lady who was recently separated from her husband, due to his being wrongfully imprisoned. She had recently given birth and it was a bitter cold evening. Rabbi Moshe Leib, putting on the clothes of a gentile peasant so that she would not recognize him, went to her in the middle of the night, carrying on his shoulder firewood he had chopped himself. He made a fire for her, and something hot to drink, and then he said *Tikkun Rochel* and *Tikkun Leah*. (Menorah ha-Tehorah, p. 51, #10)

Going for a Secluded Walk

Rabbi Nosson tells over a story about Rabbi Nachman of Breslov, when he was a youth:

The *rebbe* lived in town and had his private room where he could practice his devotions. Nonetheless, he would often walk in the woods and fields to seclude himself in prayer. (Rabbi Nachman's Wisdom, p. 305, Sichos HaRan #162)

Everything is Accepted in Advance

One summer's day, the holy Rabbi of Parisov, Rabbi Avraham, went for a walk with our master, teacher, and *rabbi*, the holy *S'fas Emes*. While they were speaking with one another, the holy Rabbi of Parisov said to the holy *S'fas Emes,* "It's very hot today." The holy *S'fas Emes* replied to him by saying, "When a person commits himself to *Hashem's* service and to the yoke of the Kingdom of Heaven, like an ox to its yoke, and like an ass to its burden, then, for an ass, even the hottest weather of the summer is cool because everything is accepted in advance." *(Siah Sarfei Kodesh*, II, p. 59, #207)

From Foe to Follower

In the town of Nikolsburg there was a very wealthy man, one of the leading men of the Jewish community, who was very much against the *chassidic rebbes*. He especially stood against the strange ways of Rabbi Shmelke of Nikolsburg. All he wanted to do was to insult and humiliate the *rebbe*.

Once, on *erev Yom Kippur*, he showed up at Rabbi Shmelke's house with the gift of a bottle of aged wine. However, it was not brought with good intentions because all he desired was to get the *rebbe* drunk. He figured, if he starts drinking now, by the time he arrives at the synagogue for *Kol Nidre* [the opening prayer] the strong wine would take its effect and he would be drunk.

Thinking nothing of it, and in order to please the man, the *rebbe* did drink the wine. As soon as he finished one cup, the rich man kept filling up another. This continued until most of the wine was depleted.

117

Seeing that his idea was working out, the *misnagid* became quite happy. He finally reached the goal he so long desired. He would show the whole community how worthless *chassidim* were; for if their leader could act in a bad way, what about the rest of them?

When the shadows of the evening arrived, the *rebbe*, as was his holy way, reached the synagogue as if he were the high priest himself, ready to do his service within the Holy of Holies. The words of the sages proved themselves, "Wine is strong but fear is stronger [and dissipates its effects]," was fulfilled with that *tzaddik* – for the fear of the Day of Judgement completely removed any effects of the wine on him.

Now the *rebbe*'s holy way was that he always spent the whole twenty-four hours of Yom Kippur immersed in prayer at the synagogue. After the evening service, the *rebbe* would stay on to recite the psalms, before the ark. He would be the prayer leader and all the congregation would repeat the psalms, verse by verse after him, in a loud voice. When he arrived at the verse [in Psalms 41], "By this I know that You have shown favor to me, if You will not cause harm to my enemy on my behalf," he repeated this verse many times, and he translated it into *Yiddish* many times. He said, "Even if I have enemies who desire my humiliation and shame, even so, forgive them – so prayed King David." The *rebbe* shouted this out many times that it should enter the hearts of those praying, and they all began sobbing and crying.

Now the *misnagid*, who was by the eastern wall of the *shul*, knew full well what the *rebbe*'s intention was when he prayed the passages repetitiously. It was a hint that he didn't want revenge against those who hated him so much that they desired his humiliation, rather, he prayed and pleaded for their welfare and success. So, moved was he at the Reb Shmelke's righteousness and humility that his heart turned inside him. He came before the *rebbe* and fell down at his feet. He started crying and begging for his forgiveness. He even confessed publicly his evil plans.

However, Reb Shmelke said to him, "You think that I accepted the office of *rabbi* of Nikolsburg for the crown and the honor. No, my friend, it is not honor that I desire. If you had indeed shamed me, how many benefits would you have bestowed upon me, by that. For how many of my sins and transgressions would you have washed clean with the shame and humiliation?" The *rebbe* repeated his words, several times, that it was too bad he had not been humiliated for drunkenness, since it would have done him great good.

Hearing these holy words, the man wept even more as he begged for his complete forgiveness.

119

Following this incident, he became a friend and admirer of the *rebbe* for all his days. (Shemen ha-Tov, p. 77, 49)

Afflictions Purge a Man of His Sins

Two years before he left this world, the Chofetz Chaim was afflicted with a severe nosebleed on the night of the *Pesach seder*. He'd lay in bed for many days like this. When one of his closest followers came to visit, the Chofetz Chaim said to him: "How good are afflictions [like his nosebleed] which purge a man of his sins. So too," he continued, "the humiliation and abuse that a man suffers in his life; for they are a substitute for afflictions that cleanse him of his transgressions. But, what a disaster it is then," he concluded, "for someone like me, who in his whole life has never been insulted!" (Michtivei ha-Chofez Chaim ha-hadash, vol. 2, II, p. 138)

Speaking with Gentleness

One of his *chassidim* writes about Rabbi Rafael of Bershad:

At times, he would discuss with us at length the importance of *ahavas Yisrael*. He explained to us, that you need to treat your fellow man as if he were your king and be gentle with him and not forceful. His son, Rabbi Levi, told over once that the *rebbe* spoke with him about some matter and he saw, while his father was talking to him, that he was as lowly as if he were a servant talking to his master. (Midrash Pinchas, p. 63)

Always Deferring When Possible

While in his advanced old age, the Chofetz Chaim called all his household together and said to them: "My children, I want you to know that all my life I was always careful not to make anyone defer to me; on the contrary, I would always defer to all and give way. I want you to know, if someone takes this path, it is good for him."

There was one time when the Chofetz Chaim was walking on a narrow sidewalk and an army officer approached him from the opposite direction. The *rabbi* instantly stepped down from the sidewalk to let him by. The officer, who was astonished to see this elderly man hasten so to defer to him, went up to him and asked him about it. The Chofetz Chaim replied, "All my life I have made it my custom to give way and move to the side so others can pass." The officer responded, "Such a custom should assure that you will pass through life in happiness." (Michtivei Chofetz Chaim, Chelek ha-Dugmaos, 35)

121

Be an Accountant of Your Soul

The son of the Chofetz Chaim recalls an event that took place while he was a young man:

"I remember how he would often go by himself into the fields outside the town to make a soul-accounting of all his actions of the day. Along with him, he took a little notebook in which he wrote his 'accounts', and the fences [rules of the extra self-restraint] which he had made for things in which he had stumbled.

A number of times, I heard from him how he wondered that people having even the smallest store keep a notebook to record their accounts, but as for the accounts of their soul, they make no effort to be aware of their situation [by having a notebook and making soul-accounts]." (Michtivei ha-Chafetz Chaim ha-Chadash, vol. 2, I, p. 7)

Accepting Beforehand

The holy Rabbi Yitzchok of Vorki was once, in his youth, traveling with one of his friends, and their wagon driver was giving them a lot of trouble. He did not want to wait for them as he felt they were taking too long to load up the wagon and all arrive for departure. They also wanted to say their prayers before embarking on the trip, and he felt this wasn't fair to him. His friend was getting into continual arguments with the driver about this, but Rabbi Yitzchok bore it all in silence with serene equanimity.

When his friend asked him how he was able to stay so composed, he answered, "You didn't prepare yourself to suffer from the wagon driver because you thought he would show you respect, and treat you well, allowing you to do as you like. You figured that you'd be able to take a lot of time to say your prayers and to act in a pious way as you want. But as for me, I'm already well familiar with the way that wagon drivers act, and how they can make their passengers miserable. So, as soon as I decide to take a trip with a wagon driver, I prepare myself in advance to bear even more than what we've gone through till now. As a result, I don't get excited or angry about what he does because I'm prepared beforehand to suffer from him even a good deal more than this. In fact, this driver still remains a veritable *tzaddik* in my eyes compared to what I expected." (Derech Tzaddikim, p. 51)

Now for some of us this practice would rid us of so much anxiety and anger. For others who already build up an unbearable anxiety in their heart, it could have a reverse effect, but the point is still an important one. Be more accepting that life has its ups and downs, and that in the end everything will work out one way or another. Don't allow yourself to get all worked up, and prepare yourself beforehand, mentally and physically to handle all tasks that might confront you. Then, things will be much easier to handle.

The Ein Yaakov and His Disciples

The Besht would often take his disciples with him in his coach on journeys. Always valuing his time, during the trip some of those with him would recite the psalms out loud or read out loud from *Ein Yaakov* [the *Aggadah* of the *Talmud*]. (Emunas Tzaddikim, p. 6, #3) The *Ein Yaakov* is really the perfect *sefer* for this; I too used to carry it with me for years during my travels. It is rather a light version of the Talmud, stories to be specific, that are perfect to think about while you journey.

Love of Mitzvos

The author of *Emunas Tzaddikim* writes about the pious actions of Rabbi Shlomo Leib of Lentshno:

I must record for a memorial what I saw with my own eyes of his great love for performing the *mitzvos*. When he held the *esrog* in his hand, everyone saw how he almost expired due to his great love for the *mitzvah*. He would kiss the *esrog*, again and again, as he chanted *hallel*. During *Succos* he placed the container with the *esrog* in it, before him on the table. He would stare at it with great love and *d'vekus*. The same thing he did with the *shofar*, which he always placed near him during the month of *Elul*. Again, and again, he grabbed it in his hands and brought it to his lips as if wanting to blow it. So too, when it came to the holy *shabbos*, when he sat at the table, he looked lovingly at the *challos*. Because of his love for the *mitzvah*, he could not contain himself, and he would even kiss the *challah*. But one time, a certain *rabbi* was visiting him on the holy *shabbos*, and when he saw this, he too took one of the *challos* of the twelve on the table and kissed it; however, from then on, the *rebbe* never again kissed the *challos*. It just didn't feel the same. (Emunas Tzaddikim p. 87)

Starting Over Again

Rebbe Nachman of Breslov often spoke about his childhood piety. He said that he began anew many times each day. He would begin the day with deep devotion, resolving that from then on, he would be a true servant of *Hashem*. Then the temptation of a tasty meal, or such would get the better of him, and he would fall from his elevated level of devotion. But on that same day, he would begin again, with new resolve toward true devotion.

125

The *rebbe* would thus fall and begin anew several times each day. He often told us how he continually began serving *Hashem* anew.

A Perfect Blessing

Rabbi Chanoch Henich HaCohen (the future *rebbe* of Alexander) was given this teaching by the *rebbe* of Tomashov:

"A *chassid* of Tomashov searches and questions himself not just once, but a second and third time, about everything he does."

"From then on," shared the *rebbe* of Alexander, "I spent much time examining, and considering all my actions, literally everything I did. When I returned home from my trip to the *rebbe*, for example, and went to have something to eat, I picked up the vessel for the hand washing and began to question myself. What will be if I do not wash my hands? And if I do wash, am I then prepared for eating? Let us say I wash my hands and make a blessing over the bread – what kind of blessing will it be? How will I let it out of my mouth, and to Whom will I utter it?

So, there I stood, examining and considering my actions, for about two hours. Now, my father-in-law [in whose house he was living], seeing me standing there, was astonished, and asked me why I did not begin my meal. However, I was silent and did not respond. Instead, I went deeper and deeper in self-examination until I had plumbed the depths completely. Then, I washed my hands, and roared in a thunderous voice that was not mine, '[Blessed art Thou, etc. who hast commanded us] on the washing of the hands [*al netilas yadayim*]!' And I tell you, since then I have never merited to give forth a blessing like that." (Ha-Admor Rabbi Chanoch Henich mi-Alexander, p. 34)

Never Fall Completely

This is an important rule in *avodas Hashem*. Never let yourself fall completely.

There are many ways that a person can fall. At times, your prayer and devotion may seem without meaning. Strengthen yourself, nonetheless, and begin anew. Act as if you were just beginning to serve *Hashem*. No matter how many times you fall, rise up, and start again. Do this again and again, for otherwise you will never come close to *Hashem*.

Draw yourself toward *Hashem* with all you're might. Remain strong, no matter how low you fall. Whether you go up or down, always yearn to come close to *Hashem*. You may be brought low, but cry out to *Hashem*, and do everything you can to serve Him in joy. (Sichos Haran, #48)

Glossary

Achdus- Togetherness

Ahavas Yisrael- Love of one's fellow Jew

Al Naharos Bavel- Psalm said about the destruction of the Temple (psalm 137)

Aliyah- Immigrating to Israel

Am Haaretz- Common Jewish man, sometimes referring to someone unlearned in Jewish laws

Am Yisrael- Jewish nation

Amen- Used after a prayer, or other formal statement to express solemn ratification or agreement

Amidah- See definition of **Shemoneh Esrey**

Amora- Their legal discussions and debates were eventually codified in the *Talmud*. The *Amoraim* followed the *Tannaim* in the sequence of ancient Jewish scholars.

Aron Kodesh- The *Torah* ark or ark in a synagogue

Aseres Hadibros- The Ten Commandments

Atik- Ancient

Aveirah /Aveiros- Sin/Sins

Avodah- Service

Avodas Hashem- Service to G-d

Avos- Forefathers

Avrechim- Married men who learn in *Kollel*

Ba'al Koreh- The individual who chants *Torah* from the scroll at the synagogue

Bar-Mitzvah- A ceremony and celebration for a Jewish boy at the age of 13 when he takes on the religious duties and responsibilities

Bedikas Chametz- Checking for unleavened bread before Passover

B'Gashmius- Material benefits from this world

129

Beis Din- Jewish court
Beis Din Shel Maalah- Court in Heaven
Beis Hamidrash/Beis Medrash- House of study, Synagogue
Bekitsche- Decorative coat worn on *shabbos* by *chassidish* men
Ben- Son
Benched- Blessed
Beruchnius- Spiritual benefits
Birkas hamazon- Blessings after eating bread
Bitachon- Faith
Blatt- Pages of *Talmud*
Bnei Yisroel- Children of Israel
Bochor / Bochorim- Young single man/men
Borchu- Blessing said during the *ma'ariv* prayer recited by the *chazan*
Boruch Hashem- Thank *Hashem*
Bracha- Blessing
Bracha Shehakol- Blessing over eating food
Bris Milah / Brisim- Circumcision(s)
Chachom- Wise man
Chalav Yisrael- Cow milked by a Jew
Chalukah- Traditionally the first hair-cut of a boy at age 3
Chas V' Shalom- It shouldn't happen
Chassan- Bridegroom
Chassid- Follower or person seeking higher purity
Chassuna- Jewish wedding
Chatzos- Midday or midnight
Chavrusa- Study partner
Chazal- Sages
Chazzan- Prayer leader
Cheder- Religious Jewish school for boys
Chevrah Kaddisha- The local burial society
Chiddushei Torah- Original *Torah* insights
Chochmah- Wisdom
Cholent- Hot Meat dish traditionally served for *shabbos* Lunch

Chovos Halevavos- A Main work in Jewish literature, **Duties of the Heart** by Rabeinu Bachya ibn Paquda zt'l

Chumash- Five books of Moses

Churban- Destruction (of the Temple)

Cohen / Cohanim- Priest(s)

Daven / Davened- Pray, Prayed

Dayan- Judge

Der Heiliker- The holy man

Divrei Torah- Words of Torah

Drush- Homiletic interpretation of the Torah

D'Vekus- Closeness to G-d

Eibershter- G-d in *Yiddish*

Ein K'Elokeinu- There is none like Our G-d

Eliyahu Hanavi- Elijah the Prophet

Emunah- Faith

Eretz Yisrael- the land of Israel

Erev- Evening before

Farbrengen- Feast made by *chassidim*

Gabbai- Aramaic (a) the person responsible for the proper functioning of a synagogue or communal body (b) an official of the *rebbe's* court, who admits people for *yechidus*, private meetings

Galil- Northern Israel

Gan Eden- Garden of Eden

Gaon- Great rabbinical scholar

Gemara- *Talmud*

Gematria- Numerical value

Gemilus Chassadim- Kindness to others

Geonim- Great sages

Gilgul- Reincarnation

Goy / Goyim / Goyishe- Non-Jew(s)- Literally means nation(s)

Hagadah- Book recited at the *seder*, on Passover night

Hagba'ah- The ceremony of lifting the Torah

Halacha- Jewish law

Har Sinai- Mountain where the Jews received the Torah

Hareini Mekabel- I accept upon myself

Hashem- G-d (literally translates as the name)

Hashgacha Pratis- Everything comes from Hashem; personal supervision

Haskama- Approbation

Havdalah- Prayer to conclude the *shabbos*

Heichalos- The Heavenly Mansion

Hiddur Mitzvah- The beautification of a mitzvah, actions that glorify, or beautify, the observances and celebrations within Jewish tradition

Hillula- Memorial

Im Yirtze Hashem- With the help of G-d

Kaddish- Prayer recited for the deceased soul

Kadoshim- Holy Sacrifice

Kallah- Bride

Kameyos- Amulets

Kapara- Forgiveness

Kavanah- Concentration, intent. The frame of mind required for prayer or performance of a mitzvah (commandment)

Kazayis- A Talmudic unit of volume, approximately equal to the size of an average olive

Kedusha- Holiness

Keili- Vessel

Kever- Grave

Kiddush- Blessing recited on *shabbos* over a cup of wine

Kiddush Levana- Blessing over the new moon recited monthly

Klal Yisroel- Jewish nation

Kohanim- Jewish priests

Kohen Gadol- Head Jewish priest

Korbanos- Sacrifices

Krias Shema- Recital of the *Shema* prayer

Ksav Yad- Personal handwriting

Lag B'Omer- A Jewish holiday celebrated on the 33rd day of the counting of the *Omer*, celebrating the end of Rabbi Akiva's students dying. It is also the memorial of Rebbe Shimon Bar Yochai.

L'Chayim- a word used to express good wishes just before drinking an alcoholic drink

L'Chovod Shabbos Kodesh- In honor of the holy *shabbos*

L'Illui Nishmas- For the sake of the deceased

Levi- 1) A descendant of the tribe of Levi, which was set aside to perform certain duties in connection with the Temple; 2) Son of Jacob (Israel). Ancestor of the tribe of Levi.

L'Shem Shamayim- For the sake of Hashem alone

Ma'aseh Merkavah- Works of the chariot

Machlokes- Controversy

Madrega- Spiritual level

Maggid- Story teller / Sometimes referring to R. Dov Ber Mezritch, Leader of *chassidus* after the Baal Shem Tov

Malach /Malochim- Angel(s)

Mamash- Hebrew word for 'really'

Manna- The food that fell from the sky to feed the wandering Israelites in the *Torah*

Marror- Bitter Herb used on Passover

Mashpia- Spiritual guide

Mashul- Comparison or parable

Mechuten- Son's father-in-law

Melamdim / Melamed- Teachers/teacher

Mezuzah- A scroll placed on doorposts of Jewish homes, containing a section from the *Torah* and often enclosed in a decorative case

Midbar- Desert

Midos- Character traits

Mikveh- Ritual bath house

133

Minchah- Afternoon prayer service

Minyan- Quorum of 10 men during the prayer service

Mishnah / Mishnayos- The first compilation of the oral law, authored by Rabbi Yehudah HaNasi; the germinal statements of law elucidated by the *Talmud*

Misnagedim- Opponents, used to refer to those whom are opposed to the chassidic movement

Mitzvos- Commandments

Mizbeiach- The altar in the Temple

Mizrach- East, designates the direction in which we should pray (from our vantage point, towards Jerusalem.

Moshe Rabbeinu- Moses our teacher, Greatest prophet who ever lived.

Moshiach- The anointed one, who will herald in a new era for Judaism and all humankind.

Motzei- Night after

Mussar- The study of character correction

Nachas- Pride or gratification, especially at the achievements of one's children

Neshamah- Soul

Niggun / Niggunim- Melody(s)

Nigleh- The revealed aspects of the Torah

Nishmas Kol Chai- (The breath of every living thing) is a Jewish prayer that is recited following the Song of the Sea

Olam Haba- The world to come

Parnasa- Income

Parsha- Weekly portion read from the *Torah* on *shabbos*

Parshios- Parchments

Pasul- Unfit

Perush- Commentary

Peyos- Sidelocks

Pidyon / Pidyon Nefesh- Redemption for the soul, in form of a note and money given to a sage

Pilpul- Loosely meaning "sharp analysis"; refers to a method of studying the *Talmud* through intense textual analysis in attempts to either explain conceptual differences between various halakhic rulings or to reconcile any apparent contradictions presented from various readings of different texts.

Posuk / Posukim- Verse, Verses

Pshat- Simplest meaning, based on the text and context

Rabbanim- Sages

Rachmonus- Mercy

Raphael- The angel of healing

Rav- Rabbi who answers *halacha* questions

Rebbetzyn- The rabbi's wife

Remez- Meaning 'hint" in reference to scriptural interpretations

Ribono Shel Olam- Master of the world/ *Hashem*

Rishonim- The leading rabbis and *poskim* who lived approximately during the 11th to 15th centuries, in the era before the writing of the *Shulchan Aruch*, and following the *Geonim.*

Rosh Chodesh Seuda- Festive meal for the new Jewish month

Rosh Hashanah- Jewish new year

Rosh Hayeshiva- Head *rabbi* of a *yeshivah*

Ruach Hakodesh- Divine inspiration

Ruchniyus'dike- See *Ruchniyos*

Schlepp/Schlepping- *Yiddish* for drag around

Schmooze/Schmoozing- *Yiddish* for talking and hanging out

Sefer / Seforim- Book(s)

Segula- Remedy or charm

Seraphim- Angels

Seuda- Festive meal

Shaaloh- Question for a *rav* to avoid stumbling on another occasion

Sha'atnez- The prohibition against wearing clothes woven of wool and flax.

135

Shabbosdiker kapota- *Shabbos* garment
Shabbos- The Jewish sabbath, a day of rest and spiritual enrichment.
Shacharis- Morning daily prayer service
Shalosh Seudos- Third festive meal on *shabbos*
Shamash/Shammes- Lit. servant. 1) The candle that is used to light other *Chanukah* candles; 2) the janitor or caretaker of a synagogue
Shamayim- Heaven
Shas Bavli and Yerushalmi- Babylonian *Talmud* compiled in Babylon, Jerusalem *Talmud* compiled in Jerusalem before the Babylonian *Talmud*
Shas- Complete order of the entire *Talmud*
Shavuos- Holiday commemorating the giving of the Torah
Shechinah- The Divine Presence
Shechitah- Slaughter of *kosher* animals
Sheker- Falsehood
Shemoneh Esrey- The central prayer of the Jewish liturgy, also known as the *Amida*
Shidduch- Dating for the sake of finding a marriage partner
Shikker- Drunk in *Yiddish*
Shir Hama'alos- Song of Ascents in the Psalms
Shiras HaShirim- A song written by King Solomon, Song of Songs
Shiur- *Torah* class
Shliach- Messenger
Shochtim- Slaughterers of *kosher* animals
Shtiblach- Small synagogues
Shtreimel- Fur hat worn during *shabbos*
Shul- Synagogue
Shulchan Aruch- Code of Jewish law
Siddur- Jewish prayer book
Simcha- Joy and celebration
Simchas Torah- Holiday Celebrating the *Torah*
Sippurei Tzaddikim- Stories of righteous people
Siyum- Party for finishing a *Torah* book

Sod- Secret of the *Torah*
Sukkos/Succah- Jewish holiday celebrated in booths
Tallis- Prayer shawl worn by men
Talmid- Student
Talmud Chachom- Wise student
Tanach- Acronym of *Torah* (the five books of Moses), *Nevi'im* (Prophets) and *Kesuvim* (Writings)
Tanna- Jewish sages whose views were recorded in the *Mishnah*, during the first and second centuries
Tefila / Tefilos- Prayer(s)
Tefillin- Holy scriptures wrapped in a box with leather straps to attach to the head and arm
Tehillim- Psalms
Teshuva- Repentance
Tikkun- Repairing
Tikun Chatzos- Lit. 'Midnight service"; a prayer recited by pious Jews at midnight, lamenting the destruction of the Holy Temple
Tishah B'Av- Memorial Day to recall the destruction of the Temple
Toiveled- Purified oneself in the *mikvah*
Tzaddik/Tzaddkim- Lit. Righteous person(s). A completely righteous person often believed to have special, mystical power.
Tzaddik Nistar- Hidden righteous man
Tzedakah- Charity
Tzetl- Note
Yechidus- Personal time spent with one's *rebbe*
Yeshiva- School for learning *Torah* for older boys or men
Yeshuah- Redemption
Yetzer Hara- Evil inclination
Yichus- Family lineage
Yid /Yiddala / Yidden – Jew(s) in *Yiddish*
Yiddishkeit- *Yiddish* for Judaism

137

Yiras Shamayim- Fear of G-d
Yom Tov- Holiday (lit. means good day)
Yungeleit/Yungerman- Yiddish for young man
Zechus- Merit
Zeide- Grandfather
Zemanim- Times of the day

Made in the USA
Columbia, SC
14 September 2018